Essential Career Transition Coaching Skills

Career moves (even positive ones) can be disruptive for the individual, and the psychological impact of changing roles or careers is often underestimated. Career transition coaching is a relatively new field, but one that is highly relevant in the modern world. In *Essential Career Transition Coaching Skills*, Caroline Talbott explores the most effective career transition coaching techniques and explains the psychology behind them.

Looking at both self-motivated and enforced career changes, the book pays particular attention to the psychological processes experienced by the client, so that the coach can understand and anticipate their reactions and help them make the most successful career moves. It covers general skills, tools and techniques that can be applied to any career transition as well as more specific examples such as moving from management into leadership, aspiring business owners and career changers. Case studies illustrating the methods of experienced coaches and step-by-step guides to coaching techniques are also included.

Ideal for those already experienced in general coaching and looking to specialize, as well as anyone whose job requires coaching skills, such as managers and HR professionals, this timely book provides a comprehensive guide to the whole transition cycle – from choosing a career direction or change, to making a move and adapting successfully.

Caroline Talbott coaches and develops leaders, particularly professionals who have progressed into leadership roles. She is also a specialist in change management and organisation development and is a qualified NLP Business Practitioner.

Essential Coaching Skills and Knowledge
Series Editors: Gladeana McMahon, Stephen Palmer and Averil Leimon

The **Essential Coaching Skills and Knowledge** series provides an accessible and lively introduction to key areas in the developing field of coaching. Each title in the series is written by leading coaches with extensive experience and has a strong practical emphasis, including illustrative vignettes, summary boxes, exercises and activities. Assuming no prior knowledge, these books will appeal to professionals in business, management, human resources, psychology, counseling and psychotherapy, as well as students and tutors of coaching and coaching psychology.

www.routledgementalhealth.com/essential-coaching-skills

Titles in the series:

Essential Business Coaching
Averil Leimon, François Moscovici and Gladeana McMahon

**Achieving Excellence in Your Coaching Practice:
How to Run a Highly Successful Coaching Business**
Gladeana McMahon, Stephen Palmer and Christine Wilding

**A Guide to Coaching and Mental Health: The Recognition
and Management of Psychological Issues**
Andrew Buckley and Carole Buckley

Essential Life Coaching Skills
Angela Dunbar

101 Coaching Strategies
Edited by Gladeana McMahon and Anne Archer

Group and Team Coaching
Christine Thornton

Coaching Women to Lead
Averil Leimon, François Moscovici and Helen Goodier

**Developmental Coaching: Life Transitions and
Generational Perspectives**
Edited by Stephen Palmer and Sheila Panchal

Essential Career Transition Coaching Skills

Caroline Talbott

Routledge
Taylor & Francis Group

LONDON AND NEW YORK

First published 2013
by Routledge
27 Church Road, Hove, East Sussex BN3 2FA

Simultaneously published in the USA and Canada
by Routledge
711 Third Avenue, New York, NY 10017

Routledge is an imprint of the Taylor & Francis Group, an informa business

British Library Cataloguing in Publication Data
A catalogue record for this book is available from the British Library

Library of Congress Cataloging in Publication Data
Talbott, Caroline.
    Essential career transition coaching skills /
    by Caroline Talbott.
      pages cm.—(Essential coaching skills and knowledge series)
    Includes bibliographical references.
    1. Career changes—Psychological aspects.   2. Career development—Psychological aspects.   3. Personal coaching.   I. Title.
    HF5384.T35 2013
    650.14—dc23   2012047574

ISBN: 978-0-415-69666-1 (hbk)
ISBN: 978-0-415-69667-8 (pbk)
ISBN: 978-0-203-36212-9 (ebk)

Typeset in New Century Schoolbook
by Keystroke, Station Road, Codsall, Wolverhampton

Printed and bound in Great Britain by
TJ International Ltd, Padstow, Cornwall

Dedication

For Jean, my mother, and Muriel, my godmother: for inspiring me with their love of education and lifelong learning.

Contents

Figures

Foreword

No man is an island. These were the wise words of English poet John Donne, who reinforced that as human beings, we do not thrive when we are isolated from others, that each of us has a role to play in mankind.

Today, these words hold true, more than ever before. Within our complex, interconnected world, our search for greater meaning and purpose, and making a greater contribution, lies beneath many deeper coaching conversations.

This is why this book comes at a pivotal time within coaching and other helping professions. To help us connect more with each other, and ourselves, to make better choices, and be energized by the sense of fulfillment and empowerment that more aligned options bring.

The lonely executive comes to mind, who suddenly finds him/herself out of a job after a very successful career, then starts to look at what *really matters* most to them, now. Or the technical expert, who has built an identity around specialist skills, who then has to 'step up' and lead others in uncharted territories.

Or anyone of us going through a major life transition – both expected and many times not. Or retirement, or moving in or out of a relationship, or dealing with a loss or new family situation; all that stretches us into areas that require us to step back, think about, and adapt to life differently.

These are just a few of the transition points our author, Caroline Talbott, takes us through. She gifts us with an eclectic blend of some of the psychological, mental, behavioural and practical factors we need to consider when supporting another around their most critical stages in their life or career.

Through these pages, she also broadens our perspective on some of the choices and resources available to us, within this emerging area, resulting in a surge of energy and inspiration to 'take action', like an excellent Career Coach will do!

One that will enable us, and those we support, to play an important role, small or large, in society and make a greater difference – whatever that may be.

Katherine Tulpa
CEO, Association for Coaching
August 2012

Acknowledgments

I would like to thank the following people, without whom this book would not be what it is. Their contributions have been many and various, ranging from reviewing and critiquing; sharing the experiences featured here; friends and family for their encouragement; my coaches and coachees for inspiration and learning – theirs and mine.

Andy Britnell, Angela Dunbar, Angela Watson, David Dodd, Deni Lyall, Elisabeth Kübler-Ross Foundation, Emma Lewis, Francesca Long, Gary Boner, Gerry O'Neill, Gladeana McMahon, Guy Buckland, Helen Harrison, Jane Kitchen, Julia Latimer, Karen Mitchell, Karen Williams, Kate Williams, Katherine Tulpa, Kirsty Harper, Lindsey Huckrack, Martin Baldwin, Peter Hawkins, Rachael Burgess, Rachael Ross, Roy Sheppard, Steve Bucknell, Sue Knight, Sunil Jindal, Xanthe Wells.

Above all I want to thank my wonderful husband Ian for the unfailing support he has given me during the gestation of this book: moral support, encouragement, cheerleading – and a lot of washing up!

Unless otherwise stated, all quotes from Deni Lyall, Peter Hawkins, Andy Britnell, Gerry O'Neill, Angela Watson, and Karen Williams are drawn from my interviews with them.

1

Why career transition coaching?

Peter Drucker, writer and management consultant, was right when he said that if you don't manage your future somebody else will. An essential truth but there's more to it than that. . . .

The working world has never been more chaotic nor presented more opportunities – for those who choose to take control. In the UK between 2001 and 2007 the fastest growing occupation for women grew by 93 percent and the fastest declining shrank by 66 percent. For men the figures were 49 percent and 39 percent (Sissons, 2011). Fifty-seven percent of 97,000 people worldwide surveyed by Kelly Services (2011a) expected to change career in the next five years. This provides a huge potential market for career transition coaches.

I was prompted to write this book when I started to look around for a resource to support career transition coaches in all the different contexts in which they work – to my amazement not one single book like this existed! Self-help books on careers abound and I found a handful of books covering some aspects of the field or a single 'formula' but none with the comprehensive scope of this one.

This book covers the full picture, including inspiring stories of coaches and their coachees, and provides a practical guide that can be pulled off the shelf whenever you have the opportunity to coach clients during changes in their careers.

This chapter starts by examining the transformation of 'career' in the twenty-first century and where and how coaches can provide support. It outlines who can benefit from using this book, the business and human case for career transition coaching and how this relates to other forms of coaching and career support. Finally it guides you through each chapter.

Context and meaning of 'career' in the twenty-first century

What is a career today, in the twenty-first century? Does it even exist? Daniel Priestley (2010) says there is no such thing! The world is changing faster than it ever has before, as are many people's expectations, wants and needs from their working lives. A 'career' can provide a whole host of benefits from the monetary to status, self-esteem, skills, knowledge, sociability, meaning and purpose. Arguably we are at a unique point in history where people's demands and aspirations have never carried so much weight in the market place and where they have never had so much influence over their working lives – if they choose and are capable of taking that power and control. Why do I believe that?

Past and present

Over the past 20 years exponential change has taken place, driven primarily by technological developments, globalization, social and demographic forces – and the pace has increased even more over the last five. Some might argue that an even more powerful force fueled economies in the decade up to 2008 – institutional and individual risk and greed; Gordon Gekko in the movie *Wall Street* proselytized that greed is good, right and works. To our cost we found that it isn't and it doesn't!

Expectations at the time of the 2008 credit crunch and consequent recession were that everything had changed. But has it? Credit is indeed much harder to come by and 'an age of austerity' has gripped most of the developed economies while growth continues in developing countries such as China and India, albeit at a slower pace. Growth is at best slow in the Western world and many jobs have disappeared or working hours have been reduced so that many are 'under-employed'; and still more is to come, particularly in the public sector with the UK, Eurozone and US debt reduction programs. And yet these (perhaps?) short-term difficulties merely overlie significant longer-term drivers of change.

The forces which shaped the world in the late twentieth and early twenty-first centuries are accelerating – changing the work that is available either at all or in particular locations. For instance the technology that created jobs, such as web and computer games designer, has also destroyed them (e.g. film processing, high street retailing) and has made it possible for work to be done in different ways, such as home working, off-shore call centers and through social media – increasingly work really *is* 'something you do, not a place you go to'.

This has led to the development of the 'knowledge economy' and 'knowledge workers'. Unhelpfully there are no universally accepted definitions of these terms but, using the top three occupational groups (managers, professionals, and associate professionals) as a proxy for 'knowledge workers', the number in the UK increased from just under 7.9 million in 1984 to 12.5 million in 2004. It is forecast to grow to 14.2 million (45 percent) by 2014 (Brinkley, 2006, 2008).

Analyzing this continuing trend in the reshaping of the economy and work force, Paul Sissons in 'The hourglass and the escalator: Labour market change and mobility' (2011), found a 'hollowing out' of the labor market, like an 'hourglass'; highly skilled and managerial jobs are increasing at the top and those with less skills and qualifications are being pushed down into low-skilled jobs, lower-wage service occupations or unemployment, as middle-range work (such as administrative, secretarial and process or machine operative jobs) has reduced. The recession since 2008 has continued and accelerated these trends.

Certainly the days of a 'job for life' are long gone in most sectors and rapidly dwindling in those pockets of the public sector where they have endured. Sissons' report for The Work Foundation urges policy-makers to 'ensure good quality careers advice is available' to enable workers to change jobs. He also recommends facilitation of skills trans-fer from public sector to private as well as re-skilling and retraining – significant opportunities for career transition coaches to support on a large scale if they work to drive such culture changes and sell the benefits of a real live coach rather than skills training alone, or a self-help book. Self-help books are widely available but working with a coach can much accelerate desired changes.

The trend toward living and working longer also has potential to increase opportunities for career transi-tion coaches as people seek changes throughout their careers – a 2011 TUC report found that in December 2010 64.9 percent of 50 to 64 year olds were in work, compared with 56.5 percent in 1992, an increase of 8.4 percent; over the same period the percentage of those aged over 64 rose from 5.5 to 9 percent.

People are on the whole better educated, better informed and better connected; according to the OECD (2011b) fewer people are failing to complete upper second-ary education and more are completing tertiary education. Between 1998 and 2009 the proportion of adults who had not completed upper secondary education dropped from 37 to 27 percent; over the same period completion of tertiary education rose from 21 to 30 percent. The long-term effects of changes to university funding and fees in the UK remain to be seen. People are better informed through easy, instant access to a wealth of information on a global scale – according to Internet World Stats, at the end of March 2011, there were 2,095,006,005 internet users (Miniwatts Marketing Group, 2001–2012).

In May 2011 Ofcom reported that in the UK 74 percent of adults had broadband access, with about 500,000 house-holds signed up to superfast broadband with a headline speed five times higher than in 2010. Ninety percent of adults aged 35 to 44 have the internet at home compared with 25 percent in 2000; 48 percent had used social network-ing sites in the first three months of 2011, up from 40 percent in 2010; and 27 percent of adults and 47 percent of teen-agers own a smartphone – 28 percent of adults use them to access the internet (up from 22 percent in 2010) and

57 percent to visit social networking sites. The pace of adoption is increasing with 59 percent acquiring their smartphone in the previous year and 37 percent of adults and 60 percent of teenagers admitting they are 'highly addicted' to their smartphone.

In its 2012 report the World Bank highlighted how mobile technology is creating new work and business opportunities across the globe. In many countries, including the US and UK, there are more than 100 cellular subscriptions per 100 people.

Twitter reported 200 million accounts in February 2011, LinkedIn more than 120 million members in over 200 countries and territories in August 2011 and Facebook more than 750 million active users in mid-2011. Google added 10 million users to its Google + social media site in just 16 days. Increasingly these social media are used to network, find business partners, recruit employees and to look for new assignments and projects. Online job boards have become the most popular way to find work – 26 percent used them to secure their most recent job according to Kelly's 2011 Global Workforce Index (Kelly Services, 2011b).

Future trends

Increasingly we are exhorted to 'be happy', with the UK government introducing a national index to measure well-being. In 2010 the Office for National Statistics (ONS) set up a debate on the subject and found that among the contributing factors were job satisfaction, adequate income and wealth, work–life balance and meaning and purpose – all of which would be significantly influenced by good career choices and transitions.

On a global scale, in 2011 the OECD launched a Better Life Index across its 34 member countries as an alternative measure of success to that of Gross Domestic Product; it includes factors such as jobs, income, work–life balance and life satisfaction.

So how does this play out in the workplace? In her book *The Shift: The Future of Work is Already Here* (2011) Lynda Gratton, Professor of Management Practice at London

Business School and in 2008 selected by *The Financial Times* as 'the business thinker most likely to make a real difference over the next decade', argues that five forces will fundamentally change the way we work over the next 10 to 15 years – she adds 'energy' to those four key factors (technological developments, globalization, social and demographic forces) which have shaped and driven change in the last decade – and points to 32 key trends that are shaping the future of work. She identifies three key shifts that she believes individuals will need to make to have a rich work and personal life:

1 Gaining 'mastery' rather than broad, general skills
2 Building deep relationships with 'your posse', regenerative and ideas people (your career transition coach?)
3 Deciding whether you want a life based around money and 'stuff' or to do work that is productive and exciting, which you feel great about.

Similarly, Daniel Priestley (2010) argues that the way ahead is to take his five steps and, most importantly, find the 'hidden theme' and 'join the dots' to being a 'Key Person of Influence', a KPI, in your chosen niche. His thesis is also that we are in an 'Ideas Economy', that everything has changed and that 'your best thinking of five years ago is your baggage today'.

Other business thinkers are also engaged in identifying likely trends over the coming years which will influence businesses and hence the working lives of those who are employed. Professor Gary Hamel, London Business School Visiting Professor, founder of MLab (Management Laboratory) and ranked by the *Wall Street Journal* as the world's most influential business thinker, wrote a blog entry entitled 'Capitalism is dead. Long live capitalism' (2010). He argues that we are at last starting to realize that our pursuit of more and more material things is unfulfilling and unsustainable and that we want a 'kinder, gentler sort of capitalism ... that understands the difference between maximizing consumption and maximizing happiness'.

This follows from the assertion in his 2007 book *The Future of Management* that the increasing pace of change presents both dangers and opportunities and that success will depend on organizations' ability to adapt and adopt new principles such as resilience, innovation and employee engagement. Fortunately the best of human spirit and qualities (such as originality, grit, derring-do) are needed to create this but these are different to the qualities on which twentieth-century management was founded (e.g. economy, orderliness, reliability).

Research reported by Groysberg, Kelly and MacDonald in 'The new path to the C-Suite' (2011) shows that capabilities demanded of those at the top of organizations are already changing; based on job profiles developed by executive search firm Heidrik and Struggles and interviews with senior managers they found that business acumen and soft leadership skills are more important than technical and functional expertise. To succeed at executive level you must be a strong communicator, a collaborator and strategic thinker with a global mind-set and ability to offer deep insights on key business decisions.

Individual, personal factors also play a part in career choices and expectations, such as temperament and life stage, as do 'generational differences'. These have implications both for individuals and for organizations. The *Gen Up report* (Penna and CIPD, 2008), whilst cautioning against 'labelling' people, recommends using generational difference to 'appreciate the variety of views in the workforce' and to address these proactively to be successful in 'the war for talent'. They identify the four key generations as Veterans (born 1939–1947), Baby Boomers (born 1948–1963), Generation X (born 1964–1978) and Generation Y (born 1979–1991) with Generation Z (born 1992–2008) about to join the workforce. They all have different perspectives on life and work. Similarly, US research (Wray-Lake, 2011) found that recent cohorts of high school seniors value work, job security and intrinsic rewards less and increasingly value leisure time.

Whilst it is important to be aware of these generational differences, this is just one of many factors to be taken into account in understanding career needs and expectations; however, it does indicate that the generations coming into the workforce are likely to have far more changes of career than their forerunners, and Baby Boomers are not untouched by this trend. As people live longer and pensions are paid later and are of less value, individuals may have, and indeed many want, to work longer than the retirement ages common in the Western world to date. Working lives will be longer and many will change occupations, some because they are simply unable to continue in their current field, others because they want to change.

In summary, there is a virtuous circle of consumer and worker demand for change in the way organizations operate which in turn will provide a more sustainable world with more satisfying careers, but for that to happen leaders and workers need to change their approach and behavior and to develop new mind-sets, capabilities and skills.

So, let us return to that question: 'What is a career in the twenty-first century?' A career is a way of earning a living, which of itself gives personal satisfaction and is part of a satisfying and enjoyable life. With the pace of global change accelerating rapidly, career opportunities are constantly changing, with some avenues closing or reducing and others opening or expanding. In future a career may include periods of employment in different organizations or different types of organization (private, public or 'social sector'); it may or may not include climbing a traditional type of 'career ladder' – although many will still choose to climb (56 percent of graduates expect to be in a management role within three years of graduating according to an Institute of Leadership and Management/Ashridge Business School joint study in 2011).

It could include periods of self-employment or no employment, such as a sabbatical, gap year or extended maternity or paternity leave, or downshifting to have less work and material rewards. Full- or part-time employment or a 'portfolio career/life' where a variety of jobs or roles are held simultaneously are equally possible. For some there will continue to be some kind of fairly well-defined 'career path', e.g. for lawyers and accountants, for many there will not. The search for more control over work as part of a meaningful and enjoyable life is likely to increase as Generations X, Y, Z and millennials move through the workforce.

These changes provide the opportunity, impetus and necessity for 'career reinvention' during a lifetime and ability to adapt to new circumstances and roles – therefore huge numbers of career transitions! The help of a career transition coach will be invaluable in helping individuals to make decisions, find opportunities in their next stage and in adapting to it. Along with those who see positive new possibilities there will be casualties who perceive that their choices and opportunities have disappeared and who will need help to pick themselves up and move on.

In my view the keys to career satisfaction and successful career transitions are adaptability, flexibility and ability to see possibilities, with a strong set of core values and beliefs (which may change over time) – in all of these career transition coaches can help.

Who will benefit from this book

This book is a resource for anyone working in a career transition coaching context and I will use the word 'coach' as shorthand to cover all of these, even though some are not formally 'a coach'. This is the go-to resource which you can pick up when you are working with anyone through a whole range of career transition points to help them find a new direction, understand and work through the thoughts and feelings they are experiencing and find the best ways of adapting to their chosen path. It is also a resource for anyone going through such a transition themselves to help them understand what they are experiencing and why they would benefit from the support and knowledge of a good coach.

It addresses the needs of the experienced through to the newly trained coach, wherever and however they are employed or deployed. It will help you support clients in making successful career moves both individually and in an organizational context, minimizing the disruption of individual and structural change in organizations through this very effective employee engagement mechanism.

Who will it benefit? Essentially four interest groups. Those who are:

1 Already working as a coach or in a coaching-related role
2 Training in coaching skills
3 Working in organizations where coaching around career transitions is part of their role
4 Planning to change career or who have made a significant change in their role or career.

These could be:

• Existing coaches wishing to undertake or specialize in career transition coaching
• Coaches looking to set up their own coaching business including or specializing in career transition
• Careers advisors/counselors wanting to broaden their approaches and skills
• Tutors and students on courses such as coaching and outplacement
• Providers of outplacement services or coaches aspiring to work as their associates or employees
• Those working in public sector agencies supporting job seekers or in private organizations servicing them
• Managers, HR professionals, resourcing or redeployment managers and others in organizations who are required to support organizational objectives by coaching individuals or groups of employees through career transitions
• Individuals who are dissatisfied in their current role, who want to make a significant change or who have been promoted.

It is a practical guide to approaches and techniques that you can use in a career transition context, a toolkit to enable you to be the best career transition coach you can be. It is not a manual of general coaching skills or approaches, although some of these can be used equally successfully in other contexts. Nor is it a 'formula' – it gives you a range of choices to suit your individual client and your own preferences and capabilities.

The business and human case for coaching in career transitions

The case for career transition coaching can be summed up as addressing these problems: ineffective managers, disengaged employees, waste of talent (people in the wrong career and not making the most of their capabilities and/or being demotivated) and misuse of human capital (people unemployed). These apply on both a business and personal level.

What is the evidence of career transition coaching's effectiveness? Case studies and personal histories of successful career change and the benefits of using a coach in the process abound but specific quantitative information is limited. In fact only 36 percent of organizations surveyed by the CIPD (2010a) do actually evaluate the effectiveness of coaching. Those which do evaluate coaching focus on qualitative evaluation, such as reaction, stories and testimony.

CIPD's 2011 survey, whilst not asking specifically about career transition coaching, found that in 33 percent of organizations that use coaching, the priority is to prepare and support people in leadership roles and in 43 percent it is to support performance management, both of which can have a career transition element.

In other research the ICF's *Global Consumer Awareness Study* (2010) found that 42.6 percent of respondents who had experienced coaching chose 'optimize individual and/or team performance' as their motivation for being coached. This reason ranked highest, followed by 'expand professional career opportunities' at 38.8 percent and 'improve business management strategies' at 36.1 percent. Eighty-three percent of respondents were 'satisfied' and 36 percent were 'very satisfied' with their coaching experience.

To make the case for specific aspects of career transition coaching:

- *Redundancy / redeployment* The case is fairly easily made and many organizations choose to use some form of career transition coaching when they are downsizing in some significant way. Coaching can help people secure a new role more quickly and get on with their lives. It also sends a positive message out to those who are retained about the company's people values and helps to reduce 'survivor syndrome'.

To quote one of Deni Lyall of Winning Performance's clients who had initially tried to go it alone: 'I was doing a lot of things but now I know the *right* things to do that will get me somewhere'.

- *Movement into management / leadership* What is the cost of job changers, due to promotion or any other reason, taking a long time to adapt to their new role? Again no specific figures are available although it's possible to infer that there is a productivity cost, for instance, Macleod and Clarke's report 'Engaging for Success' (2009) found that highly engaged employees try 50 percent harder and perform 20 percent better while disengaged employees cost UK business £40 billion pa. A manager who is either on a long and steep learning curve or under-performing through failing to adapt will be unlikely to be engaging their staff.

  Another measure of success is provided by the views of colleagues working with executives who have received coaching. In research by Erik de Haan and Christiane Niess (2011) to assess the organizational impact of coaching, 72 percent of those asked were able to identify a significant moment of change which they believed was due to coaching – all but one were positive.

- *Organizational restructuring* Equally, from what we know of transitions from models such as Bridges' (2004, 2009), transitions can be paralyzing if not managed well – at both individual and organizational level – and coaching, team or individual, can help enormously in adapting quickly and thus cost-effectively.

- *From education to first career steps* It is also an investment that has traditionally been made, to a greater or lesser degree, for those in education, particularly in higher education although the approach has been more one of 'guidance' rather than coaching. (See below for the similarities and differences between career guidance/advice/counseling etc. and coaching.)

- *Individual career changes* All the above benefits apply equally to individuals, to which can be added the financial penalties of constantly changing jobs leading to periods of unemployment, having to start again at the bottom of the career ladder, failing to prepare properly for self-employment leading to business failure or the cost of retraining if changing careers completely. The real question is, will your epitaph be 'I wish I'd spent more time in the office?' or is there something bigger out there calling you? (*The Hero's Journey*, Dilts and Gilligan, 2009).

One of the most important benefits would be to enable a 'quick start' with minimum disruption and greatest early success in a new chosen direction, e.g. self-employment. Individuals are willing to invest large amounts on their physical appearance and well-being (e.g. holistic therapies, or spa and pampering weekends), why not in their mental and career well-being?

Evaluation of coaching benefits and results

Potential clients may ask, 'Why use a coach? There are huge numbers of self-help books out there' or 'Surely this is just "life" isn't it – I can figure it out for myself'. I think the answer to this is, why get help learning to do anything new? If you were going to learn to kayak you would not just get a book, read it and then assume you could get in a kayak on your own and navigate your way expertly and safely down a river. Also our education generally teaches us knowledge but doesn't teach us how to think, make decisions about our personal lives or how to manage our emotions – emotional intelligence (Goleman, 1996, 1998) – especially through times of pressure and change.

Organizations are increasingly realizing that customers don't want to just be left to their own devices and it's the same with their careers – why should employees and other 'consumers of career' be left to work it out alone? Most businesses provide help desks for their customers and others give the option of 1:1 support e.g. PC World has the 'Tech Guys' who will help you get going with what you have bought! It's false economy in terms of time and mistakes to expect to just muddle through on your own and hope you'll pick it up quickly – the career transition coach will help you work out what you need to know and do, as well as how to achieve it. The benefits for organizations are enormous.

Evaluation of coaching interventions is an area where we can lead the field as career transition coaches – there is plenty of scope for improvement! CIPD's *Real-World Coaching Evaluation: A Guide for Practitioners* (2010b) provides a framework for evaluating coaching in organizations, which you can use to formulate a business case which will hit the right note for a potential new client or as part of your marketing materials. This is covered in more depth in Chapter 8.

A focus on career transitions

The focus of this book is 'career transitions', that is the stages and transitions in an individual's *working* life, some of which are self-motivated and some of which are generated by forces outside their control. It is not about life transitions, which are the subject of another book in this series (Stephen Palmer and Sheila Panchal's *Developmental Coaching: Life Transitions and Generational Perspectives*, 2011). Its purpose is to provide the career transition coach with a good understanding of the process and psychological impact of career transitions, including choosing or losing a role as well as adapting to it, with coaching approaches and techniques which can be used in these circumstances. It also gives an overview of the different contexts in which career transition coaches work to help coaches make an informed choice about the route or routes to take in developing their own practice and niche. And finally it covers what it takes to be a successful career transition coach with a reminder of the critical factors in any coaching practice.

It draws on both theory and practice and includes real examples from practicing coaches of how they have supported clients.

Relationship with other types of career support and coaching

Two questions are often raised: first, what is the difference between career transition coaching and other forms of support that are available to help with their careers? And second, how does it differ from other types of coaching?

Types of career support

These mostly go under the titles of guidance, advice or counseling but in recent research (Yates, 2011) there seem to be no formally accepted definitions of each, although the essence of each could be gleaned from what is said about them in literature. There are both similarities and differences in the approaches and they vary in how they are practiced by different institutions and practitioners.

The important thing as far as this book is concerned is that it is very firmly within the coaching camp, focusing on 'partnering with clients in a thought-provoking and creative process that inspires them to maximize their personal and professional potential' (International Coach Federation) or 'a collaborative solution-focused, results-orientated and systematic process in which the coach facilitates the enhancement of work performance, life experience, self-directed learning and personal growth of the coachee' (Anthony Grant, 2000, quoted by Association for Coaching, 2012).

Relationship with other forms of coaching

Again, there are no hard and fast rules here; career transition coaching may be provided as part of other forms of coaching (e.g. executive, business or life/personal) or it may be a defined niche within which a coach works (as recognized in the Association for Coaching's definitions on their website). Equally it may be a part of the remit of an outplacement organization, HR department or manager.

Once again, as far as this book is concerned, the focus is on career transitions although the coach may have a broader remit in working with the client.

This book is organized as follows:

Chapter 2: Understanding your client and career transition points

The purpose of this chapter is to give an understanding of who your client is and how you can help them together with an overview of the points of career transition at which clients may seek or need your help, from choosing a new role or career through to adapting to it successfully and quickly.

By the end of this chapter you will know how to use Robert Dilts' (Dilts, Grinder, Bandler and DeLozier, 1989; Dilts, 1990; Dilts and DeLozier, 2000) (neuro)Logical Levels to understand your client and where they really need or want help. You will also appreciate the stages of career transition and how you can support a client through them with different interventions, approaches and tools, as well as how to apply some well-known coaching models in the career transition context.

Chapter 3: Psychological factors in career satisfaction and transition

The purpose of this chapter is to give the coach an understanding of transition and change as a process rather than a single event and the value a career transition coach can bring to a client in this. You will also understand how personality impacts on career satisfaction and transition. It will show how you can help your client understand and work their way through it, the reaction you may get which may seem less than positive, and also to understand the effect this may have on you in working with them, especially if their experience is one they perceive as negative, such as redundancy.

Some well-known models and theories such as Kübler-Ross's (1973 [1969]) change curve are used, as well as other tools and tips to help you and your client transition successfully.

Chapter 4: Making career choices

The purpose of this chapter is to describe the steps in making a career choice and provide you with tools and techniques you can use in each. Much thinking these days is short term and people may question the benefit of thinking longer term. I would argue that it's even more important to understand what your values are and what motivates or demotivates you or you are in danger of becoming a serial job/career changer, not to progress but to rectify the mistakes you have made. After reading this chapter you will appreciate the importance of helping the client not just to 'choose their next job' but really help them to find long-term satisfaction in their career by understanding themselves better and looking beyond just the next role and how they can bring in some money as quickly as possible. You're looking to help them make sustainable choices which will motivate and enthuse them.

Again you will know how to use a range of approaches and tools to help them achieve this.

Chapter 5: Getting there

Here I look at the practical work that will help the client achieve what they want – preparation and search for their new role, be it employment or self-employment or perhaps retirement. It will cover how a coach can help in practicalities such as CV preparation, interview skills and helping clients understand their strengths and transferable skills as well as the psychological preparation, for instance building confidence and a new sense of identity.

Chapter 6: Challenging transitions

This chapter looks at the more challenging aspects of career transition – the situations you might encounter and the approaches used by successful career transition coaches. It includes challenges relating to the type of transition itself (for instance redundancy), personal characteristics (such as older workers or those with no work experience) and psychological or behavioral challenges.

Chapter 7: Transition into a new role or life

Often it is not appreciated that finding a new job or setting up a business is just the start of another career transition, the transition into a new role or even a new life – it may seem the transition is complete but there is a whole new world to adapt to at this point, with both practical and psychological implications. This chapter examines how you can help your client adapt quickly and successfully.

Chapter 8: What it takes to be successful as a career transition coach

There are many business models for the coach wishing to practice career transition coaching and it is also a useful skill for those working in organizations in broader roles such as HR or line management. By the end of this chapter you will understand the pros and cons of each to help you in making your choice.

Chapter 9: Final word: Vital considerations

Here I reinforce essential tenets underpinning coaching such as coaching ethics and contracting and the importance of training, CPD, accreditation and supervision.

This book contains rich and diverse stories demonstrating how skilled and inspiring coaches have helped individuals to take control of their careers, to create the life they want, and spurred organizations to really live their values and brand; it will rouse you to develop your own career transition coaching practice and give you methods and tools to turn that into a reality. All the cases are real although sometimes names and other details have been changed to protect the person's identity.

There has never been a better time to make a career in career transition coaching, with people wanting and expecting more meaningful and fulfilled working lives, and global trends making changes both necessary and possible.

Read on and let this book inspire you to take the next steps in your own career transition.

Understanding your client and career transition points

So why would anyone want career transition coaching? And how and when could you support them? Where would you start?

In the changing world the first chapter describes, this one looks at what spurs individuals to seek career transition coaching, plus gives an overview of the help they look for and that you could provide. Often you will need to look beyond the obvious and probe to find out what the client really wants, as they may be unconscious of or completely unaware of their deeper needs or what you can actually do to help them. Sometimes it can be a bit like the doctor's surgery – someone comes to you with a specific request, you build some rapport and trust; question, listen and discuss; and then just before the ten minutes of the appointment are up the *real* need becomes apparent. Or it may take far longer into the coaching relationship before you find out everything that could make a fundamental difference to your client. Of course, career transition coaching is just like any other type of coaching in this regard – the main difference in my view is that there is also often a narrow and simplistic view that it is just about careers guidance or outplacement; that is, it's about choosing a career after university or about companies buying outplacement for redundant employees to soften the blow. I see it far more broadly and as a process, a transition or even a transformation, not just a point in time, which impacts people and organizations at many points in a working life and is particularly significant in the context of leadership and management.

In my experience the simplistic view of career transition coaching often leads to it being undervalued – and consequently underpaid! Traditionally it has been mainly the preserve of women in Careers Guidance and Advice services and all that this means for equal pay. Outplacement coaching is also regarded as lower status than leadership and executive coaching so this is key in deciding your niche and how you present your services.

We in the career transition coaching profession should be promoting this wider perspective for a number of reasons, for both clients and the coaching profession.

For clients:

- Many more people at all stages of their life and careers can benefit from our support – enabling them to be happier and more successful, whatever that means to them
- Organizations benefit through reduced costs as managers and leaders become effective far more quickly in their new roles – reducing costs of mistakes, and making them and their team more productive in less time.

For the coaching profession:

- It's a business growth opportunity
- It's a chance to enhance the status and reputation of career transition coaching which tends to be labeled with the traditional, low status and low monetary value occupation of 'career guidance' and 'career advisor'.

Career transition points

These are what I see as the main transition points and the areas in which we can support individuals during each:

- *Education to first job* Identifying their talents and what they want in a first job and how the two things match up; understanding what's available; understanding and doing what they need to do to get the job they want, e.g. getting work experience, interview practice.
- *Career change* Identifying what they want in their career; identifying transferable skills; understanding

what's available; understanding and doing what they need to do to get the job they want, e.g. networking, adapting their CV.

- *Promotion to a higher level* Individuals seeking promotion and then adapting to it – considering what's required at the new level; the skills they have and skills gap; testing out their reasons for wanting promotion and what it will give them; CV and interview preparation. It's particularly useful in helping new managers and leaders adapt to their new role – these people can be responsible for large teams and often have little or no support in adapting to a new status where what they *do* is less important than *who* and *how* they are.

- *Redundancy/redeployment* As well as needing help with similar challenges to those above, people facing redundancy or redeployment are likely to have emotions such as anger, sadness and shock about their situation, and their self-confidence and self-esteem may have been damaged. Often there may be pressure on them from the organization they work for to find a new job – especially in the case of redeployment when the company will want the value of their 'resource' realized and used most gainfully.

- *Self-employment and portfolio life* Coaching can help individuals decide whether this really is for them; it can help them identify skills gaps and how they can transition and adapt successfully once they have made a decision.

- *Return from a career break* Again the need to identify transferable skills and opportunities to use them in the job market can be accompanied by a need to develop confidence and self-belief.

- *Retirement* This is a huge psychological as well as physical change and the better prepared an individual is the more happily they will adapt and be able to make the most of what should be a positive change. The impact on the individual and the coaching they need will be different depending on whether the choice is theirs or that of the organization they work for, or possibly due to other circumstances such as ill health or physical incapability to carry on with full-time permanent work.

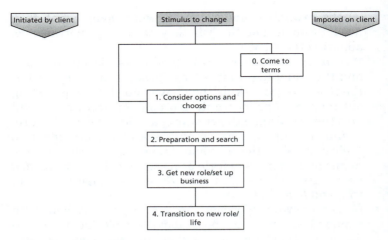

Figure 2.1 Career transition journey

The career transition journey

These are the points in these transitions where coaching can play a critical part: see Figure 2.1.

What are the likely challenges you will be dealing with at these stages on the career transition journey?

- *Stage 0: Coming to terms* Dealing with strong emotions such as anger, shock, denial, sadness, mourning, lack of confidence
- *Stage 1: Consider options and choose* Broaden choice, challenge assumptions, create vision, identify talents, set goals
- *Stage 2: Preparation and search* CV and interview preparation, networking, personal branding and 'pitching', confidence and self-belief
- *Stage 3: Get new role/set up business* Preparation for first 100 days – business and personal vision and objectives
- *Stage 4: First few months and transition to new role/life* Successes, challenges, new identity and style, crystallization of new approaches, capabilities and skills, adapt to a new reality.

How can you help on the transition journey?

Here is a summary of approaches and tools you can use at each stage of career transition which are included in the later chapters of this book. My aim is to give you a toolkit you can pick up and use easily with a client; these are approaches that either I or other experienced career transition coaches find particularly helpful.

Transition point	Approaches and tools
0. **Coming to terms:** dealing with strong emotions such as anger, shock, denial, sadness, mourning, lack of confidence	Kübler-Ross' (1969) change curve, Prochaska's stages of change, Bridges' *Managing Transitions*, review past successes, listen, hold up a mirror, reframe, use of metaphor
1. **Consider options and choose:** broaden choice, challenge assumptions, create vision, identify talents, set goals	Vision and dream, career satisfaction drivers, values identification, Well Formed Outcome, Clean Language, Logical Levels, psychometrics and personality profiles, wheel of life
2. **Preparation and search:** CV and interview preparation, networking, personal branding and 'pitching'	SWOT, wheel of work, information sources, identity shifting, Logical Levels, preparation of interview answers, mock interview, Cognitive Behavioral Coaching, visualization, anchoring, decision making
3. **Get new role/set up business:** preparation for first 100 days – business and personal vision and objectives	100 day plan, SWOT, priorities including quick wins, stakeholder analysis, Logical Levels, assess the business, team, self
4. **First few months' transition:** successes, challenges, new identity and style, crystallization of new approaches, capabilities and skills, adapt to a new reality	Kübler-Ross change curve, hierarchy of leadership, emerging leaders, seven transformations, timeline, unlearning, Logical Levels, leadership pipeline, identity shifting

Figure 2.2 Transition journey approaches and tools

This is how the process generally works for Karen Williams of Self Discovery Coaching and author of *The Secrets of Successful Coaches* (2011):

- Consultation over the phone and agreement of coaching 'package' – usually three months or six sessions
- Meet fortnightly, agree contract, complete wheel of work, agree goals
- Identify values and beliefs, coach around these as required
- Plan what they want to have achieved by the end of the coaching contract
- If they want or are facing a significant career change complete SWOT and skills audit. At this point it may be necessary to re-examine their goals in the light of this new information
- Complete CV
- Once know type of job desired start job research – e.g. who do they know, appropriate recruitment agencies, networking, job sites, publications
- Interview skills
- Personal barriers such as confidence, self-belief, esteem
- Getting back on track if things are not going as expected.

Overall approaches

Framework for coaching

An overall framework for your career transition coaching is essential, just as with any other coaching intervention. Your usual favorite – such as GROW, that is 'Goal, current Reality, Options and Will' (Whitmore, 2009) or CLEAR, Contract, Listen, Explore, Action and Review (Hawkins and Smith, 2006) – may serve the purpose very well, although many outplacement organizations have their own proprietary approaches which you would use if working for them.

Coaching approaches I find work particularly well for career transitions are NLP, using metaphors, and particularly Robert Dilts' Logical Levels (Dilts and DeLozier, 2000). You will find that this book owes much to them as I find them exceptionally powerful. This is how you can incorporate them into your coaching.

Neuro Linguistic Programming (NLP):
'The study of excellence'

Many people have a 'love it or hate it' attitude towards NLP (Bandler and Grinder, 1975) depending on the exposure they have had and that can apply equally to you as a coach or to your clients. There are many excellent NLP trainers and practitioners who use it with positive intent to empower themselves and others but it also has a sort of 'celebrity' or 'cult' wing which can be seen as, and in some cases *is*, manipulative and damaging.

My own experience of NLP has been absolutely life enhancing – it is NLP that enabled me to transform my life by setting up my own business, and to improve my relationships with my 'significant others'; in my coaching it has enabled my clients to improve their relationships and ability to deal with everything that life throws at them. This is part of a testimonial from a client I worked with in their transition from a singleton professional to senior manager:

> I have greater self-awareness, more confidence and more time. Caroline's coaching has enabled me to see that, whatever problems or issues I face at work or in my private life, I can find a way to address them. I have . . . an invaluable set of tools which have made me more productive and more capable.

The definition of NLP I use is 'the study of excellence'; for Sue Knight, with whom who I trained as a Business Practitioner, it is 'the difference that makes a difference' (Knight 2009). NLP is founded on observation, recording and codifying how successful people do what they do so that those 'skills' can be passed on. I have put 'skills' in inverted commas because excellence is most likely rooted in beliefs and identity rather than 'capabilities'. It is about how to lead a successful and happy life. We are continually learning from our experiences, consciously or unconsciously, throughout our lives – NLP enables us to do that more consciously, systematically, effectively and positively. For instance, you may work for a manager you don't get on with and resign from your job feeling angry and depressed. What can you learn from this? You can *choose* to learn any number of things on many different levels. You could look for the differences in beliefs and values that caused the rift (I had a manager who one day 'jokingly' revealed that he saw himself as a slave driver and his team as the slaves!); you could think about organizations where you would find people with values more in keeping with your own (perhaps a social enterprise); or you could 'reframe' it and look for the 'positive intention' of this experience – maybe that it's made you realize the importance and strength of your own values and given you an opportunity to find somewhere you really *love* working and not just somewhere you go to earn money. You can choose *that* learning or you may just take away some potentially damaging learning such as 'I'm no good', 'I'm weak and hopeless', 'I'll never get another job now'.

For me NLP is simply a way of life, a powerful toolkit which enables you to harness and enhance excellence in yourself and others. I use it both consciously and unconsciously, for instance in preparing for coaching sessions or meetings. I deliberately use NLP tools to get me into the right frame of mind and if something happens which triggers a negative and unhelpful thought I find myself mentally 'reframing' it. For example, when meeting someone who is behaving negatively and defensively, my first reaction may be to dismiss them or react equally negatively. Now I find myself quickly and unconsciously 'reframing' to wonder what's causing them to behave like that: I show empathy and try to understand things from their point of view. Usually their behavior changes quite quickly.

Like any toolkit it should be used with positive intention. If you haven't been trained in NLP, the tools I have included in this book will give you some practical approaches you can use in career transition coaching, or indeed in any other coaching you undertake – including of yourself! It is not essential that you train formally in NLP to use them and in fact you will find if you read any book on coaching skills that many of the approaches and techniques they contain are either things which are formalized and named in NLP or they are specific NLP techniques but not labeled as such. McLeod's *Performance Coaching* (2008) is an example of the latter, containing many useful NLP approaches. Others are less obvious, for instance 'focusing a client on what they want, in other words "maintaining direction" and "developing goals"' (Starr, 2008). GROW (Whitmore, 2009) or CLEAR (Hawkins and Smith, 2006) start with developing a strong idea of what the client wants to achieve. The NLP version of what the client wants to achieve is a 'Well Formed Outcome' (WFO) (O'Connor and Seymour, 2003).

In NLP, preferences for 'away from' and 'towards' thinking are recognized (Knight 2009); many people have a natural tendency towards the former and in some occupations are purposefully trained to think in this way, that is, to look for faults, e.g. engineers or auditors. Those whose preference or training is for 'away from' thinking often find it difficult to focus on what they actually want and talk a lot about what they *don't* want to happen. Usually they are completely unaware of this until you draw their attention to it.

If you *do* have negative preconceptions about NLP I would ask you to do exactly as you would ask your coachees – keep an open mind, use the techniques wholeheartedly and judge them by the results and outcomes. With your coachees you don't need to label your techniques – just do it!

The references in this chapter provide excellent further reading and you have the option to attend a good training course.

If you have trained in NLP I won't need to convince you, you already know! For you this book will highlight tools and approaches that work particularly well during the career transition process.

Let's start with one of these, (neuro)Logical Levels, one of the most versatile tools which can be used for so many different purposes. Here I will show you how to use it to get to know your client quickly and deeply.

Getting to know and understand your client: Logical Levels

What it is and why it works

This is an incredible tool and you'll find I use it throughout the career transition process, for instance to discover a leader's values and style and how those can play out in their career move, or to discover limiting beliefs and develop more helpful ones. It creates a holistic view.

Robert Dilts (Dilts, Grinder, Bandler and DeLozier, 1989; Dilts, 1990; Dilts and DeLozier, 2000) developed this model based on the work of anthropologist Geoffrey Bateson (1972). The beauty of it is that it is simple to understand and its impact is profound. It enables you and your client to examine the surface levels of their environment, behaviors and capabilities as well as the hidden part of the 'iceberg' – their values and beliefs, their identity and their wider purpose in the world which influence and drive those surface manifestations.

To paraphrase Einstein, you can't solve a problem with the same type of thinking that created it. For instance, to change behavior and capabilities you must work with your client at least at the level of their values and beliefs or changes will be at best superficial. See Figure 2.3.

Overview

Begin by explaining that this is a technique to help you and them understand quickly and more fully what they are looking for and what is important to them. You will ask them questions in a particular sequence about what has brought them to you and what they are looking for. You can show them the diagram at Figure 2.3 and describe the levels, starting with environment. Some of the things they say as a result of your questions will already be obvious to them but you can expect that they will also gain some new insights which will help them get the most out of the coaching.

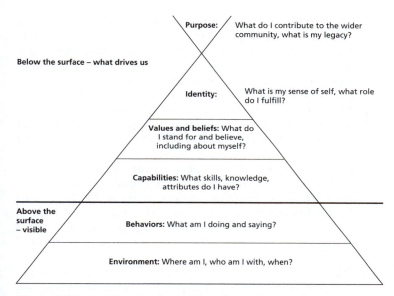

Figure 2.3 Logical Levels – based on Robert Dilts' model

Logical Levels step by step

1 Agree the topic for the Logical Levels exploration as something along the lines of their 'desire for career transition coaching' – agree the topic with them.
2 Ask the following questions, developing them based on the client's answers as you think appropriate:

   a *Environment* what is it about your current environment that has prompted you to come to me (environment is everything outside the individual – it may be where they work, who they work with, when they work)?
   b And what kind of *environment* do you want to work in?
   c And what kind of *environment* would be best for you and me to work in (this may be the location, venue, or atmosphere of the coaching)?
   d *Behaviors* What is it about what you currently do and say that's brought you here? Keep this question broad

and let the client think about it quite deeply if they need to – it may be things about their current role, it may be that they said to themselves when they were 20 that they would run their own business by the time they were 30. That is the beauty of the model – it brings out what's important to the client.

e And what do you want to be doing instead?

f And what *behaviors* from me will be particularly helpful to you – what sort of things would you like me to do and say?

g *Capabilities* What is it about your skills, knowledge and personal attributes that has brought you to me?

h And what *capabilities* are you looking for from me? Skills, knowledge and personal attributes.

i *Values and beliefs* What's important to you about this? What do you believe about yourself and your career? And about coaching?

j *Identity* How do you see yourself? How do you describe yourself? (They may say, e.g., wife and mother, teacher, engineer.) Anything else? (Ask this in order to find out all the different identities they have, and which are most important to them and for what reasons.)

k And what new *identity* are you looking for?

l *Purpose* What's your wider contribution to the world? What would you like your legacy to be? What would you like people to say about you?

3 Read back their answers working your way through the levels, starting with Purpose, and give the client the opportunity to add anything else which now occurs to them.

4 The client may find some or all of these difficult to answer. Ensure you give them plenty of space and encouragement to answer and reassure them that it is fine if they don't have answers now, as these are things you will continue to come back to during their career transition. This will then inform your subsequent coaching sessions.

5 After the meeting, type up the key points on the template at Figure 2.4, using their words as much as possible, and send it to them for their agreement as a working document.

Purpose:

Identity:

Values and beliefs:

Capabilities:

Behaviors:

Environment:

Figure 2.4 Logical Levels – client template

Pros

- Really effective way of quickly getting to understand your client and to find areas for further coaching
- Gives the client new insights
- Gives you an agreed working basis
- You also can use Figure 2.3 to develop your own philosophy to give to clients along with their contract so that they have a sense of what it will be like to work with you.

Cons

- I can't honestly think of any!

Top tips for success

- Develop strong rapport, gain the client's trust
- Give them plenty of time to think but reassure them that it doesn't matter if they don't have answers now – this is the whole point of the coaching, to help them find answers to these important questions.

What's the challenge?

- Client may struggle to answer some of the questions, especially those at the deeper levels – give them time, encouragement and reassurance
- Some may think it's a bit odd – ask them to stick with it and trust your experience as a coach about what works
- Your own degree of confidence in using this – use it on yourself, practice, and if possible ask an experienced NLP coach to take you through it as a coachee initially.

Additional options

You can ask the client to find a place in the room to physically walk through the levels. If you do this you should walk beside them so that they sense that you are with them rather than just taking notes and perhaps judging them. This can work especially well for clients who are 'activists' (i.e. who like to learn and take in information in an active and practical way) or who are kinesthetic (i.e., who process things through their senses rather than visually or auditorily (by sight or sound).

Use of metaphors and imagery

Another technique I recommend is the use of metaphors and imagery. Why is that? Imagine you have a long writing task ahead of you that is going to take you months to complete, you're going to have to fit it in between all your normal work and other responsibilities, and you're probably going to have to rewrite it many times. Then when you've finished people are going to criticize it and you'll have to go back and rewrite yet more of it!

Or, see in your mind's eye a tall ship in full sail on the high seas, plowing through the ocean waves under a blue sky on a voyage of discovery. Who knows what possibilities there are out there? Exotic places to visit – colorful sights, mysterious sounds, tantalizing smells. . . . And people you've never met before who hold secrets you never dreamed of. . . .

Which of those is more motivating? Unless you get seasick or just like to stay at home it will be the second! And that's the power of metaphor – that's the image I have as sit down each day to write this book. It could be a daunting task but an inviting metaphor ensures that every time I sit down at my computer I look forward to another part of that journey – and not only does it motivate me to write, it improves the quality of my writing because I feel a frisson of excitement about what I'm about to share with you.

This is why I believe in the power of metaphor in coaching. Again, it can be used in many contexts and it helps you and your client understand and change their 'inner world' – for instance, let's look at some recent clients thinking about the barriers they might encounter on the way to achieving their goals. One saw a high wall and imagined themselves punching a hole in and knocking down that wall. Another imagined the barriers as hurdles which she could jump over. Yet another saw a pane of glass where they could see everything they wanted almost in their grasp just the other side of the glass. When they made it tangible in this way they realized that in fact the barrier was not very big and they could just walk round the side of it!

Why it works

Our understanding of the significance and power of metaphor comes primarily from the work of David Grove (Grove and Panzer, 1989), which has been developed by practitioners such as Penny Tompkins and James Lawley (2000), Wendy Sullivan and Judy Rees (2008), Carol Wilson (2007) and Angela Dunbar (2009). Lakoff and Johnson also explored metaphors in their 1980 book *Metaphors We Live By*.

David Grove, a New Zealand psychotherapist, created what he called 'Clean Language' which he used to elicit and develop his clients' metaphors in a therapeutic context. He went on to develop other related techniques of 'Clean Space' and 'Emergent Knowledge'. Penny Tompkins and James Lawley worked with David Grove to 'model' (another NLP term!) his approach and from this they developed their own – 'Symbolic Modeling'. Metaphors are increasingly recognized as fundamental to human thinking and experience (Lakoff and Johnson, 1980): we constantly talk in metaphors, and as a coach it's enormously useful to pay attention to these for the hidden gems they contain. We 'throw in' ideas, we 'kick them around'. We see 'dark clouds ahead' or 'light at the end of the tunnel'.

Grove, Tompkins and Lawley developed a range of specific questions to ask and Tompkins and Lawley a structured process which they found worked best. Once again you can read more and train in these techniques but you don't need in-depth knowledge to benefit your client by noticing and drawing their attention to and then exploring and developing their *positive* metaphors, or by helping them to find new positive metaphors which will be useful to them.

How to use metaphors

Questions you can use which help a client find and develop a metaphor:

If you hear them use a metaphor:

- Is there anything else about (*use their words*)?
  (To help them notice more about their metaphor)
- What kind of (*use their words*) is that (*use their words*)?
  (To get detail, qualities, descriptions).

Or if they are talking about something that you think it would be helpful to make more tangible ask first:

- That (*use their words*) is like what?
  (To encourage them to think of a metaphor.)

(And yes, I do realize that saying something is *like* something else is actually a simile rather than a metaphor!)

To help them take things forward and focus on an outcome:

- And what would you like to have happen?
  (In the context of that metaphor.)

An example:

Client: I'm just so confused; I really don't know what to do. I feel as if I'm at a real crossroads in my life.

Coach: And you feel as if you're at a crossroads in your life. What kind of a crossroads is that crossroads?

Client: Well ... it's in the middle of nowhere and I can't see where any of the roads end up so they all feel like a step into the unknown.

Coach: And what does each of those roads represent?

Client: Well ... one of them is my current job. I don't know what will happen if I stay here doing this. Another is the promotion I've been asked to try for – I don't know if I really want that. The third is should I leave, get another job? Start my own business? Go freelance?

Coach: Would it help to take a walk down each of those roads and find out what's down there?

Client: Yes, yes it would. (*excitedly*) How could I do that?

Coach: Well we could do that now. You can take a walk down each in your imagination and think of where it might lead. Which one would you like to start with?

After the exploration of each road, use the metaphor to develop a goal.

Coach: And what would you like to have happen?

Client: I'd like to walk confidently down the road to becoming the orchestra conductor (*getting the promotion*), knowing that my real desire is to bring a group of talented individuals to a place where they act as one to turn a complicated piece of music on a page into a breath-taking masterpiece (*lead a team to success*).

And so you take the client down each road. You can use the Logical Levels model to guide the questions you ask, i.e. first about the environment, then what they are doing and saying, what's important about that to them and so on.

A word of caution if you are not experienced in Clean Language – if the client has a negative metaphor *do not explore it deeply*: help the client to turn it into a positive one. For instance, if they are in a dark tunnel and someone has turned out the light at the end, ask them where they would like to be instead or explore ways of getting out, making the assumption that there *is* another way out. To turn a negative 'problem' metaphor into a positive 'solution' metaphor you can ask:

- And what would you like to have happen *instead of* (*use their words*)?

I should stress that what I've used here is based on Clean Language but is not a pure form of that or Symbolic Modeling – it's a guide to use if you are not trained or experienced in these. Clearly if you *are* trained in those you would use the process as you have learnt it.

Top tips for success
- Focus on the positive and what they *do* want, getting the client to turn negative metaphors into positive ones
- Let the client come up with their own metaphor, do not impose yours.

What's the challenge?
- Keep your language 'clean' – just ask what it's like – do not ask what it looks, sounds or feels like or you will 'contaminate' your client's thinking by imposing your own thinking preference of visual, auditory or kinesthetic processing on them (O'Connor and Lages, 2004)
- Some clients may struggle to find a metaphor – to help them you can ask what they see, hear or feel. As a last resort offer them one of your own.

Pros
- Metaphors are part of everyday life, people use them all the time so they are readily accessible
- They turn intangible concepts into tangible objects or experiences, which makes it more real for the client and easier to find solutions
- They provide something that the client can return to easily to maintain their motivation and understanding
- Many people enjoy looking for metaphors and describing things in this way.

Cons

- Some people do not enjoy metaphors and find it difficult to identify them
- A negative metaphor should not be dwelt on – turn it quickly into a positive one of what they *do* want, not what they don't.

Developing your skills in using metaphor

Practice this for yourself by

- Noticing metaphors in your own and other people's everyday speech (including reading this book!)
- Deliberately developing metaphors when you talk about things
- When someone describes something ask what it's like, which encourages them to come up with a metaphor.

For further reading see the reference section and for training in Clean Language I recommend Angela Dunbar at Clean Coaching. Her website (http://www.cleancoaching.com) includes details of her distance learning programs and free resources including taster teleclasses.

Key points from this chapter

- There are key transition points in a career where you can support a client – education to first job, career change, promotion to higher level, redundancy/redeployment, self-employment and portfolio life, return from career break, retirement.
- These each contain elements in which your intervention can help move your client forward quickly and in a focused way: coming to terms with an enforced change, considering options and choosing, preparation and search, getting a new role/setting up a business and the transition of the first few months.
- NLP is a life-enhancing and powerful toolkit for use in career transition, in particular Dilts' Logical Levels (Dilts and DeLozier, 2000).

- Logical Levels can be used for many purposes during the transition; here it is used for getting a deep understanding of your client quickly and giving them new insights; also for asking questions about a client's metaphors.
- Metaphors can provide a strong means of motivation and new understanding for your client.

Let's move on now to examine and understand how personality impacts career satisfaction and transition and the psychological process of career change. It is inevitable that there *will* be bumps, twists and turns, even switchbacks in the road and by understanding these you can walk with your client and help them reach their destination as quickly and painlessly as possible.

Psychological factors in career satisfaction and transition

This chapter focuses on two aspects of the psychology of career transition:

1 how a person's personality impacts their career transition and career satisfaction
2 how career transition is likely to impact *anyone* who experiences such a change

Its objective is to help you understand your client as an individual whilst also appreciating 'normal' reactions to change so that your interventions are as helpful and appropriate as possible. At the same time you will gain insights into your own reactions as you work with your coachee.

This will enable you to anticipate and handle the challenges and support your clients in moving forward as quickly and easily as possible. Without this understanding you may be making interventions that are not going to work at all for a particular client, or at that point in their transition. You could be wasting your time and theirs and possibly damaging your relationship.

In relation to personality I will look at research findings and on psychological transition I will take you through three models classically used in understanding change. These are:

1 The Kübler-Ross change curve
2 The transtheoretical model of behavior change, commonly known as 'Prochaska's stages of change'
3 William Bridges' transitions model.

Personality, career satisfaction and transition

Imagine Clare and Sarah. Clare is an extrovert, always delving into novel ideas and looking for new experiences. Sarah is an introvert who likes to have a plan and to know what she will be doing this time next week. Who is likely to be more satisfied with their career, to find transition easiest or to come to you for support? More on Clare and Sarah in a minute.

Being aware of the potential impact of your coachee's personality on their career satisfaction and experience of transition can help you and them anticipate some of the challenges, although it should not be viewed as an absolute, immutable determinant. Everyone is different and awareness is of course the first step in changing something, should you choose.

There are of course many models and theories of personality and you may have your own favorite. Here I will look at research into some well-known ones and how they relate to career transition.

Three pieces of research (Judge, Higgins, Thoresen and Barrick, 1999; Boudreau, Boswell and Judge, 2001; Seibert and Kramer, 2001) demonstrate the relationship between career satisfaction and the 'Big Five' personality traits (the Five Factor Model – FFM):

1 Openness (curious, imaginative, inventive, independent, love variety)
2 Conscientiousness (organized, thoughtful, goal-directed, disciplined)
3 Extraversion (motivated by human interaction, enthusiastic, gregarious, talkative, assertive)
4 Agreeableness (sympathetic, compassionate, trusting, supportive)
5 Neuroticism (anxious, nervous, sensitive, self-blaming, prone to emotional instability)

(Costa and McCrae, 1985; Digman, 1990; John, 1990)

Their findings vary in detail but they consistently found that neuroticism correlates negatively with career satisfaction whilst the latter two studies found that extraversion associates positively.

Partly in response to contentions that the 'Big Five', whilst being robust, are too broad, Lounsbury, Loveland, Sundstrom, Gibson, Drost and Hamrick (2003) conducted an investigation of personality traits in relation to career satisfaction. They undertook their own field research and also reviewed earlier enquiries into the subject. They discovered that three personality traits consistently related to career satisfaction:

1 Emotional resilience
2 Optimism
3 Work drive.

These are akin to some of the key concepts of Emotional Intelligence (Goleman, 1995), particularly optimism and emotional management. Lounsbury and colleagues concluded that the three traits might serve as broad predictors of career satisfaction.

Gattiker and Larwood (1988, 1989) found career satisfaction to be a central factor in career success – if you want to be successful in your career you have to enjoy it!

So how does this relate to career transition? These traits of emotional resilience, optimism and work drive are the very same ones that will sustain and motivate individuals through a career or any other significant change in their lives. Lounsbury and fellow researchers specifically mention that these are related to adapting to a wide range of work roles, career changes, stress and uncertainty. Equally, neuroticism is not a helpful attribute in dealing with the unpredictability of job searching or of setting up a new business.

In a practical sense this is certainly so according to Karen Williams of Self Discovery Coaching. Karen uses DiSC personality profiling (Marston, 2002 [1928]) with her clients and she finds those with a high score in 'S' (Steadiness), who value security, are most resistant to change.

An insightful coach can pick up the key traits from listening to the client and it can be helpful, though not essential, for them to complete a questionnaire and receive a personal report.

And what of Clare and Sarah? Clare sets off effortlessly on the path of career change but may struggle when the going gets tough and may need strong support to be focused and disciplined in her search. Sarah may agonize for months or even years before deciding to change, having a greater fear of the unknown than the agony of the present. However, once she's decided to move she will be disciplined and organized in her search. Her next test will be the stress of the uncertainty of the outcome of her efforts. So different parts of the transition are likely to be harder for each of them. Who will come to you for support? Again they may each have different motivations initially and the extent of the support they need with different aspects of the transition will vary, and will challenge you in different ways.

Which brings us neatly on to:

Models of change

Again there are numerous theories and models of change which have their origins in different situations such as organizational change, damaging personal habits (for instance, drug addiction, smoking or problem drinking) and even death and dying. Their use has been extended over the years to encompass personal change more broadly and it is simple and straightforward to apply them to career transitions. What they all have in common is that whatever the nature of the change – whether it is chosen or imposed – there are a number of stages which will be experienced and some of these can be very challenging.

As a reminder, here I will look in detail at three of these:

1 The Kübler-Ross change curve
2 The transtheoretical model of behavior change, commonly known as 'Prochaska's stages of change'
3 William Bridges' transitions model.

The Kübler-Ross change curve

Elisabeth Kübler-Ross (1969), a Swiss doctor, originally developed the model to explain the process of coming to terms with impending death and grieving for loss. It has since become a well-established way of understanding reactions to significant change or loss, both individually and organizationally. It is a foundation of change management. It is widely recognized that it applies to unwelcome and enforced changes but is less well recognized for those that have been eagerly sought and anticipated. And of course this can come as an unwelcome surprise to those who are unprepared.

You would readily expect a client to react badly to being told they have been made redundant but would anticipate someone newly promoted or having just found a new job would be elated. But this initial feeling of optimism is quite commonly followed by the same sort of feelings as someone losing their job.

What is the Kübler-Ross change curve?

Many different versions have been developed over the years, which is not surprising as Elisabeth Kübler-Ross saw it as a model or framework, not a linear process and everyone will experience grief or change in their own individual way. It helps to have this framework in mind so that you can be mindful of what you are seeing in front of you or might expect to see.

I'll discuss firstly the five stages identified by Elisabeth Kübler-Ross and then look at how they would map on to the stages of career transition. The five stages originally identified are Denial, Anger, Bargaining, Depression and Acceptance, but in change management these are often regarded as three stages:

- Stage 1: shock and denial
- Stage 2: anger and depression
- Stage 3: acceptance and integration.

In Figure 3.1 I have given an example of how the model can apply to positive changes.

Stage 1: Denial

The individual will consciously or unconsciously refuse to accept that the change is really happening as a natural

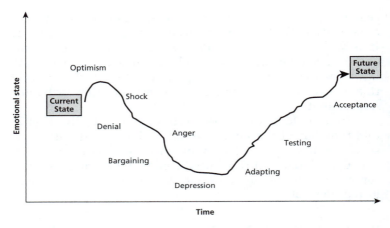

Figure 3.1 Change curve – after Elisabeth Kübler-Ross

defense mechanism; perhaps the final decision has not really been made that they are redundant, they believe there's been a mistake, or they just totally ignore it. A colleague of mine, when our Department relocated to an office in another part of the city initially refused to accept this. For weeks he went to the old office and sat at his old desk even though the floor we had occupied was completely deserted and unheated. Some people can remain locked in this stage for a long time, although usually with enforced career changes there is a point when it can no longer be completely denied, when the desk has to be cleared.

Stage 2: Anger

An individual's anger may be manifested in many different ways – it may be directed at others, at a particular person, especially someone close to them, or at themselves. It may be openly expressed or held internally.

Stage 3: Bargaining

At this stage the individual may start to look for how they might do a deal, for instance to lengthen their period of notice, or to look for another job internally. This is a way of hanging on to what they have and a refusal to give up on it; there may be hope, there may be a way, they reason. Usually this is not a strategy that will work because the decision *has* been made and it's not in their control.

Stage 4: Depression

The lowest point comes when the reality sinks in and that the situation cannot be changed. The degree of depression varies enormously from person to person – anxiety, self-doubt, feelings of sadness, crying, fear, regret, uncertainty, apathy, isolation, remoteness are all possible. At its extreme it may lead to clinical depression or even suicide.

Stage 5: Acceptance

With the realization that the change is inevitable comes a new desire to look forward. Hope and optimism and a search for new possibilities and opportunities; energy, motivation and focus return.

Figure 3.1 shows how these stages might play out during a self-motivated change, which normally begins with optimism. For a negative or enforced change just leave out the optimism stage. As the individual moves down the left-hand side of the curve, resistance to change sets in. Again, this can take many forms – it may be passive (failing to turn up for coaching, failure to complete agreed actions, lethargy, busy-ness with other things) or active (refusing to take any action, arguing with feedback or reflections back, outright anger that they find themselves in this position).

I well remember when I was an Organization Development Consultant running several projects and finding everything extremely hard going and then while describing the change curve to someone else I realized that this was affecting me – all the projects were at the bottom of the curve, the people involved putting up the deepest resistance, both the recipients of the change and the project teams themselves. This insight alone made me feel far more positive and gave me the confidence to keep on going, knowing

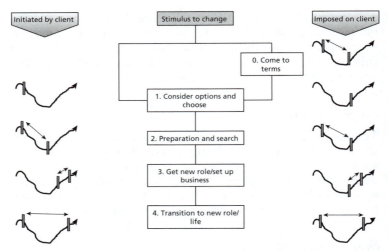

Figure 3.2 **Career transition points and the Kübler-Ross change curve**

that this was an inevitable part of the change and that it *would* pass provided we kept working towards our goal.

How long the change curve lasts varies from person to person as does its course – the good news is that your coaching is one of the things that will help them negotiate it quickly and successfully – a huge benefit of and selling point for career transition coaching.

This is how the change curve is likely to play out in your career transition coaching:

How to deal with the stages of the career transition journey

Stage 0: Coming to terms with imposed change. Someone who has just been told they are to be made redundant, or of some other change in their career which is not of their choosing, is likely to be somewhere on the left side of the change curve when they come to you, experiencing shock, denial or anger.

They will need some time and space to process these emotions, either with you or outside the coaching – developing rapport and empathy will be particularly important, without being sucked into collusion with their 'plight' or being patronizing. A listening ear, and explaining and showing the change curve to them so that they understand what they are currently feeling and likely to feel as time goes by can be very helpful. They may cycle around these emotions; perhaps having expressed anger they will go back into shock and denial. Your role is to give them a safe space to express their feelings if they wish to while finding ways to help them move on in a productive way. Whilst it's important to acknowledge these emotions it's not productive to wallow in them over a prolonged period.

Helpful things to say and do:

- Listen rather than try to convey information to them
- Acknowledge their legitimate emotions, listen and empathize
- Explain the change curve
- Ask them what are the significant things they will lose as a result and they will mourn – tell them that this is normal and understandable
- What are the significant things they will be *glad* to lose – no doubt not everything was perfect!
- Ask what would be helpful from you at this point
- Reframe. Reframing is a specific process which is part of the NLP repertoire. In simple terms it involves the person changing their perception of what has happened to them and therefore its meaning. For instance, regarding your redundancy as a personal rejection, or a sign that you are 'not good enough', is not helpful long term. Getting your client to reframe the meaning will give them power to move forward and sustain them in future – they might reframe it as 'just what happens in business', 'wrong place at wrong time' or 'an opportunity to get some money behind me and do what I have always wanted to' – whatever is right for them.

Stage 1: Consider options and choose. A client who is prompted to come to you of their own volition, thinking positively about the possibility of a new career, is likely to be at the Optimism point of the change curve. They have taken the first courageous and definitive step to doing just that and have high hopes of what they can expect from you! You can develop your understanding of them and establish their objectives with Logical Levels (Dilts and DeLozier, 2000 – see Chapter 2) and start them on their journey of career transition – the approaches in Chapter 4 will be key. You can expect that this optimism will not be maintained constantly through the transition – as they come up against challenges and dilemmas they are likely to move through the change curve. For someone involved in an enforced change, starting to consider and make choices about their future will be the start of adapting to the change and testing out their options. The same tools and approaches as mentioned above will be appropriate.

Stage 2: Preparation and search. This is probably the most testing time for the client (and their coach) as they are now focused on what they want and get down to the hard work of achieving it, perhaps experiencing some setbacks such as not being invited to interview for a job, or finding it stressful setting up their own business (dealing with unfamiliar financial matters or complicated legislation). This may also be the time where deeper issues become apparent and can be worked on, such as limiting beliefs (restricting ideas they have developed about themselves, others or how things work) or lack of self-confidence. Karen Williams of Self Discovery Coaching often finds that by session three (of her normal program of six) clients, especially women, are experiencing strong emotions or frustration. She finds it is then helpful to talk about change models such as the Kübler-Ross change curve.

Also keep them focused on positives such as their vision, what they have achieved against their measures of success and their strong skills and attributes whilst acknowledging their challenging feelings and working with them on these deeper issues – see Chapter 5 for more help on how to do this.

Stage 3: Get new role/set up their business. Here they will be adapting, testing and accepting. This is normally a period of increasing confidence and optimism when they are offered a new job or the excitement of their new business becomes a reality. They are making plans, and imagining what it will be like. This is where both they and you will experience the fruits of the hard work and difficult emotional times – worth celebrating! You will also be reviewing what has led to this success so that these lessons can be carried forward by your client for the rest of their life. For instance, what strengths have they discovered and developed, what practices do they now have for keeping focused on their vision, what strategies do they have for maintaining their resilience or dealing with setbacks?

That said, it will not necessarily be all positive, as with one of my clients, Michael. Having been offered a step up in a new organization he started to see all the positives in his current position and all the negatives in the new one – he had spent a lot of time and effort building relationships and developing his influence with senior people and putting systems in place which he felt were just about to bear fruit and enable him to make real value-adding changes; he feared he would have to start the same process all over again in the new organization. Michael knew about the change curve and wanted to check whether this was just a normal part of the emotional cycle of transition or whether he really had made 'the worst mistake of my life', as he put it. This is also very characteristic of Bridges' 'neutral zone' – see below. For the full story see my case study of Michael in Chapter 4.

Stage 4: First few months of transition to new role or way of life. This is where it all starts all over again! There is an old joke about a man who goes for an interview and is whisked by glass elevator to the executive suite, offered the finest coffees and refreshments from around the world and generally treated like a lord. He gets the job and is elated. He can't wait to start. He goes to the front door of the building and is told that this is the client entrance; he must go round the back. He can't get into the right floor because he doesn't have a pass and when he does he's asked to sit in a shabby reception area all alone for half an hour. Eventually someone comes in and says, 'Sorry, we didn't know you were coming today', and shows him to a cold and dingy office down a long lonely corridor. 'I don't understand it,' he says. 'When

I came for the interview I was treated like a lord.' 'Ah yes,' says his companion, 'but then you were a recruit, now you're just an employee.'

Admittedly it's not usually as bad as this but quite often a role or an organization does not live up to its initial promise or even if it does, after an initial period of optimism and enthusiasm reality kicks in, life intervenes and also the learning curve. New relationships need to be built, skills developed, a different style of working found, a new identity forged; perhaps a crisis of confidence or 'imposter syndrome' (Clance and Imes, 1978) and the sheer hard work of building a new team if you are a manager or leader. Once again you will be coaching through the stages of the Kübler-Ross change curve as well as the practicalities of adapting to the new status and identity – for which see Chapter 7.

Whilst I find the Kübler-Ross change curve enormously useful I thought it would also be helpful to give you another couple of perspectives on personal change, as I do believe you or some of your coachees may find some easier to relate to than others.

Prochaska's stages of change: The transtheoretical model of behavior change

The model was developed by James O. Prochaska and colleagues at the University of Rhode Island in the late 1970s and 1980s in relation to changing health behaviors such as smoking or over-eating and published in the book *Changing for Good* (1994). Over the years its use has been extended to understanding personal change more generally.

It encompasses six stages, although these are not linear and individuals may revert back to an earlier phase or abandon their change efforts altogether.

The stages are as follows, with a commentary of how I see them applying during career transition:

Stage 1: Precontemplation (not ready to change)

The person is in a job or position they don't enjoy and have no intention to change but, rather, complain about their situation and talk about all the reasons why they are 'stuck' there. Whilst you can ask them questions to challenge their assumptions and prompt them to think differently, they are not ready for career transition coaching (they may *never* be) so be careful not to take on 'bad business' or be drawn into colluding with their way of viewing things.

Stage 2: Contemplation (getting ready to change)

Here someone will start to think about making a change, balancing the pros and cons. They are still not ready to act. You can share stories of successful career transitions, including your own, and help them consider how they could reduce the risks of change.

Stage 3: Preparation (ready to change)

People at this stage are ready to start taking action within the next few weeks and are talking openly about changing. At this point you can really start to help them move forward and they may be ready to sign up for coaching. Show them how it could work for them in terms of benefits and the actual work involved.

Stage 4: Action

This is where the main work of the career transition coach takes place and where you will use all the approaches and tools in this book to support your client.

Stage 5: Maintenance
Stage 6: Recycling or relapse

In career transition this is the point at which they have achieved their goal, or at least the next stage of their long-term ambition, perhaps by getting a new job or promotion. However, it takes considerable effort to maintain the change during these stages and both internal and external support systems are important to keep moving forward.

Most career coaching will have ended at the point where the individual gets the job or even before this if your contract is for a specified number of coaching sessions.

The support of a career transition coach is particularly important at stages 5 and 6 for individuals moving into management or leadership where they are responsible for a team as well as themselves. Indeed, this can be the point at which an executive or leadership coach is actually engaged. Take a look at Chapter 7 for the full details of how you can help here.

Finally, let's look at:

William Bridges' managing transitions

It isn't change that's the problem it's the transition, according to William Bridges who distinguished between the two, identifying change as the external and transition as the internal, psychological process. Real change cannot happen without psychological transition. Although he's talking mainly about organizational change this applies equally to personal change. It is all very well getting a new job as a manager but do you see yourself as a manager? Is that your new identity, can you let go of being 'one of the boys'? Paradoxically, doing something new has to start with an ending, a letting go.

Bridges identified three stages of transition – the ending, the neutral zone and the new beginning.

Stage 1: The ending

At this stage we need to help clients recognize and deal with their loss as well as what they will gain. People often overestimate the value and benefits of what they are losing, especially when they are making a change against their will. In the film *Truly, Madly, Deeply,* Nina is grief-stricken over the death of her boyfriend Jamie and remembers only the deeply loving bond and how wonderful he was. Jamie comes back as a 'ghost' and his appalling behavior with his friends starts Nina questioning the memories of her perfect relationship until she is finally able to move on with a 'normal' man.

Stage 2: The neutral zone

This is the time in between, when the old has gone but the new isn't fully established. This is when the psychological adjustments take place and the reason it is so important to support your client in preparing for their new life, job or career so that they don't slip back into their old being and give up on their ambitions. This could not be summed up better than in the title of an article by Plimmer and Schmidt (2007): 'Possible selves and career transition: It's who you want to be, not what you want to do'.

The danger in this phase is that they may start to think about giving up and it might be easy to mistake some of the thoughts and behavior they exhibit here as 'typical' of them or symptomatic of their personality type, rather than characteristic of the neutral zone or the bottom of the Kübler-Ross change curve. Yet another reason that it's important to understand the models! What do I mean by that? A lack of confidence may be triggered by the sense of uncertainty and is not usual for this particular client – which is also particularly unnerving for them because it's an unfamiliar feeling. So coaching around finding what it is that triggers this emotion is important to find the root cause and help them find relevant strategies for them and their situation, not general 'confidence building'.

Your skill as a transition coach comes in here as you get under the surface of what is going on and really support them with the psychological transition and not just the physical transition – that's the easy bit!

Stage 3: The new beginning

This is the phase when they complete the transition into their new role and is the reason I've included 'preparation and adjustment to the new role' in my definition of career transition. This is why they need to focus on their first, say, 100 days and actively continue to work on themselves as well as the job as they deal with their triumphs and challenges.

Models of change and timelines

To help you see how these three models inter-relate, Figure 3.3 shows how I see them along a timeline. This is not to scale – the length of time the client spends at each

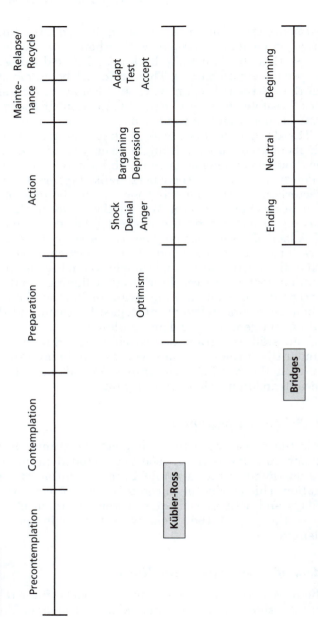

Figure 3.3 Timeline and models of change

stage varies; this diagram is just intended to illustrate where the stages fall in relation to each model.

Case study: Mark

Mark, a highly motivated and values-driven director had been working with the board of the small company he had joined recently to develop a new strategy and branding, despite the resistance of the CEO in particular. As part of this repositioning he was expecting to have a bigger and more influential role and to see a change in direction more in keeping with his values. After an initial period of hard-won consensus he found the CEO and his allies fighting a rear-guard action; some analysis I helped him work through showed that this was a power struggle he would not win. With a very heavy heart he handed in his resignation.

The role, identity and life he had envisaged over the coming years had suddenly evaporated and a huge gaping hole was left in its place. He was left mourning what might have been, what he had expected to be . . . . I helped him to understand these feelings by talking about the Kübler-Ross change curve and Bridges' managing transitions. He then understood his deep feelings of loss and was able to allow himself to recognize that he needed time to acknowledge this before he could move on. There was also some 'bargaining' going on, as he started to think about how he could perhaps continue to work behind the scenes with one of the other directors who was in tune with his views and perhaps rejoin later if the CEO left.

Discussing these models also helped him to see that he was in transition in several other areas of his life, which was compounding his sense of confusion and loss. At this point he didn't know how to answer that perennial question 'What do you do?' – we are so much defined by what we do rather than who we are. We looked at the strengths that had brought him to the successful place he'd reached, which would be important things he would take with him into the next phase of his life and this transition.

The first tentative steps towards his new beginning came with an exploration of a broad vision of how he'd like things to be in six months' time. Within a short time he began to feel at peace with what had happened and to explore options which really played to his strengths and values.

When and how to introduce a change model

Personal change is not linear, with sharp boundaries between the phases; everyone's emotions are personal and the length of time they take to work through them varies enormously. However, your intervention should help to speed up the transition and make it less painful. How you position the change models and which you use with your client is unique to your relationship, but the timing is probably best when you sense the transition is starting to have a psychological impact on them. For someone in outplacement this will probably be right at the beginning, for someone seeking a career change it may be when they start to get frustrated with a lack of instant success. If you mention it too early they will not realize how and why it has any relevance for them; too late and they will already be struggling; not at all and you are leaving them to worry about both the feelings they are experiencing and that they are peculiar and unique in having them. They should know that what they are going through is perfectly natural and normal.

If you have been engaged as a coach by an organization rather than an individual you may want to ensure that the person who has hired you also understands these models and the progress that those you are coaching are likely to make through the stages and thus manage your client's expectations. Many HR managers may be fully aware of them but it's worth introducing them into your client management discussions. It will also benefit them to appreciate the wider organizational impact of the changes they are undertaking – there could even be a business opportunity there if you are experienced in change management.

Other models of change

Other models of change are available! Those examined above are the ones which I and other coaches have found most significant for us and our clients.

Examples of other models of change you may wish to research further are:

- *Fisher (Revised 2012)* The Transition Curve model of personal change – thirteen stages based on Personal Construct Psychology (PCP) or Personal Construct Theory (PCT). This proposes that we must understand how the other person sees their world and the meaning they attribute to things if we are to communicate and connect well with them.
- *Beckhard (1969)* Three conditions which must be present: dissatisfaction with the present, a vision of the future and the first steps to achieving it must be clear and achievable.
- *Nicholson (1984)* Theory of Work Role Transitions – examines work role transitions and relationships between personal and organizational outcomes. He proposes how outcomes are influenced by the characteristics of the person, the role, and the organization and the implications for changing patterns of adjustment over a working lifetime.
- *Lewin (1947)* A three-stage model of unfreeze, change and (re)freeze.
- *Kotter (1996)* An eight-step process for leading change.

Interplay of personality and change

How do these two things inter-relate and how can you tell which you are dealing with? By listening to and talking to your client and by developing a rapport with them you will get to know them and understand what is driving their behavior and attitudes. Just asking them what has brought them to you and about their career to date, with insightful follow-up questions, will give you a good understanding, if you listen to both the content and how it's described. As suggested in Chapter 2, using Robert Dilts' Logical Levels can help speed up your knowledge of them. Or you can ask them to share a previous personality assessment or complete one for the first time.

Pay attention to the language they use and how they describe their experiences and what they want in future. What sort of words do they use and how do they describe things? Is there victim language such as 'must', 'have to' or 'should'? Notice patterns in their life and career, for instance, are their job changes self-motivated or imposed? Does their current demeanor seem different to what they describe of their past? How has change affected them previously? It's easy enough to recognize signs of the 'Big Five' (openness, conscientiousness, extraversion, agreeableness and neuroticism) in what they tell you and how, although you may need to cross-check, to ensure you are not confusing, say, the depression or anxiety phase of change with neuroticism.

Key points from this chapter

- Research and experience show that personality traits are correlated with career satisfaction and transition. Emotional resilience, optimism and work drive are correlated with positive perceptions and experiences whilst neuroticism has the opposite effect.
- Switching career involves a psychological transition which the coach should be aware of and be prepared for their client to experience. Your role is to help them handle the psychological impact of their journey (such as anger or loss) and appreciate that it is normal, as well as the physical dimensions such as skills identification and CV preparation. You can also expect to be affected yourself by your client's emotional state.
- Models of change from various origins can help you and your coachee understand this. The Kübler-Ross change curve, Prochaska's stages of change and William Bridges' transitions are particularly helpful.
- Even in positive, self-motivated change, challenging emotions are likely to be experienced at some stages of the transition.
- One of the coach's greatest skills is in judging when a client will most benefit from a particular intervention: when to listen and empathize or when to move on; being able to get under the surface of what is being presented and understand what is part of the psychological transition and what are deeper, broader challenges for the particular client and more to do with their psychological make-up.

Making career choices

Taking a holistic approach

> I'm amazed! I've spent hours filling in questionnaires
> and being analyzed . . . and in just half an hour you've
> shown me exactly what I want to know.
>
> Ursula

How many people are satisfied with their job? Shockingly,
but perhaps not surprisingly, only 37 percent according to
the Chartered Institute of Personnel and Development
(CIPD, 2012). Of course this is partly to do with their experience in the workplace but also influenced by the choices they
make about their career both at the outset and during their
working lives. People are limited by what they know about
and the majority setting out on and changing their careers
look only at the sort of jobs that they, their friends or family
are aware of. Looking through job adverts online or in newspapers, it's a process of elimination where they rule out
things that 'are not for them' (for instance, they don't want
to work in an office, they don't have the qualifications or are
not clever enough). These are to do with their own and other
well-meaning people's limiting beliefs, things they believe to
be true, which are often adopted from their parents without
question and which stop them getting what they want and
deserve (Bandler and Grinder, 1975; O'Connor and Lages,
2004).

Individuals do, of course, use varying strategies for
making career decisions but most are very restricted in their

scope and are not holistic in a way that will help them to create the type of life they want. This is not surprising given that most of our decision making is flawed, being no more than a post-event rationalization of what happened (Libet, Elwood, Wright, Feinstein and Pearl, 1979) or even merely a reflex (Bohm, 1994). Careers decision making is no different. John Lees (2011) argues that energy should be put into exploration and enquiry rather than decision making. Our job as career transition coaches is to help them think differently and 'strike a good deal, not just accept the next thing that comes along'.

'Begin with the end in mind' was Stephen Covey's second habit in *The Seven Habits of Highly Effective People,* first published in 1989 and still helping to keep him at number two in the 2010 list of 25 Top Leadership Gurus (www.topleadershipgurus.com). He acknowledged that this could be applied to many different aspects of life, and that choosing a career or careers throughout your life is fundamental to the life you have and the legacy you leave. Know what you want and you will find a way to get there. Just as with any journey, if you don't know you want to go to Colchester you won't get to Colchester – and you won't know when you arrive there anyway!

Approaches to making good career choices

Many approaches have been developed by those in the business of helping individuals make career choices through their books, such as John Lees, or outplacement specialists (e.g. Penna and Connect) who have developed their own proprietary methods which they can either license you to use as a coach, or you can work with them as an associate. And indeed most individuals have developed their own ways of deciding although they may not be conscious of what these are (Lees, 2011).

I have found the following four building blocks most useful in helping someone to choose the right direction for them; together they initially expand the person's thinking and then help them to focus:

Figure 4.1 Career decision steps

Working from right to left, end to beginning, in keeping with Stephen Covey's habit, the first logical step is to 'vision and dream', to help them discover what they want; second, they need to identify their career satisfaction drivers – the things beyond the actual content of the job which will make them happy. The third step is to establish or examine their values to ensure that any career idea is in keeping with what is important to them; finally, they must develop a Well Formed Outcome (WFO) (O'Connor and Seymour, 2003) which will ensure they have thought through how they will get what they want.

Clients will come to you at different points along their career transition path and with different mind-sets so you will need to decide the appropriate starting point as part of your contracting with them – it's not necessary to work through from one to four in that order. For instance, many of my clients who are looking to decide the next stage in their career come to me because they are dissatisfied with their current role or employer. For them it's usually most helpful and productive for our relationship to start with 'career satisfaction drivers' because that is where their focus and energy lies. And one of the important tenets of coaching is to go with the client's energy.

In my experience, even when someone says they already know what they want to do and just need help achieving it, it is still worth taking them through some or all of these steps, as few people will actually have expressed what they want in a way that inspires and motivates them and you may uncover some blind spots they will need to be aware of. For instance they may be focusing more on what they *don't* want and/or the next job rather than taking a longer term view, which will just mean they find themselves in the same position again in a few months' or years' time. This 'away from' thinking or other blind spots may be worth exploring in a later coaching session as it will impact on their future success, making them less likely to achieve their goals (Knight, 2009). Inspiration and motivation are what will keep them going when times get tough in their transition so it's really important they find that through their coaching with you.

Step 1: Vision and dream

Figure 4.2 Career decision steps – vision and dream

If you don't have something big and exciting to work towards, some Big Hairy Audacious Goals (BEHAGs) (Collins and Porras, 2000), it's certain big and exciting things are not going to happen in your life. One of your challenges is likely to be opening all your client's senses to the possibility of what their life and career could really be like, or maybe exploring why they want what they've told you they want. The best technique I have found for doing this is Visioning or Visualizing. I prefer to call it Visioning because 'Visualize' for me implies that it is just to do with a visual image, whereas what I am talking about is creating a vision of the future with all your senses.

Visioning: What it is and why it works

Visioning, or 'Guided Fantasy', is the process of helping your client to create a vivid mental image of what they want. (Bandler and Grinder, 1975) It is a very powerful tool for making a goal tangible and motivating and is widely used in many contexts, both personal and business.

The stronger the vision the client has, imagined with all their senses, the stronger will be the pull and motivation for them to have it (Knight, 2009). To really desire something you have to have some idea what it's like and this can be created initially by the unconscious mind – it doesn't need to be a real experience for the mind to know about and believe in it, as the mind can't distinguish between a real and strongly imagined event. The unconscious can also be a far stronger motivator than the conscious mind and will find ways to achieve things when logic often cannot, especially when metaphors are developed and made tangible (Grove and Panzer, 1989). How many times have you slept on a problem and found that a solution comes to you in the night perfectly effortlessly? That is your unconscious mind (Dilts and Gilligan, 2009; Rosen, 1991).

Visioning, along with positive affirmations (Jeffers, 2007) and other techniques in this book, can strongly increase your client's ability to achieve what they want.

There is no more powerful way to understand a technique that to experience it 'on the receiving end' so here is a simple visioning exercise you can do for yourself if you have not used visioning before.

Visioning exercise

Think of a food or drink you have never had but would love to try. Imagine that you have it in your mouth now, at this moment, savor it, really sense it, close your eyes . . . strongly imagine the taste, the smell, the texture, what it feels like in your mouth, what it reminds you of, how it makes you feel. Are you wishing you were eating or drinking it right at this moment? How strong is your desire to have it right now on a scale of 1 to 10? You'll find that the more strongly you imagine it, with all your senses, the stronger your desire to have it, and even to imagine you are tasting it right here and now.

Now think again of that food and savor it as before – the more often you do this and the more vividly you imagine it the more readily it will come to mind and you'll be able to imagine what it is like even though you have never eaten it.

Visioning is easier for some people than others so if you find this difficult, start by using a food or drink you *have* tried and imagine eating or drinking it as above.

Using the visioning technique in career transition coaching

Overview

Begin the process by creating rapport and trust and helping your client to relax. It works best if they close their eyes. You then ask them a series of questions about their imagined work and life, getting them to experience more and more detail so that it seems real for them. You then 'bring them back into the room' and get them to 'shake it off'. Repeat the process so that it is just as vivid. Repeat this several times if necessary so they can recall it at will at any time. You can read more about the technique in books on NLP, such as Sue Knight's *NLP at Work* (2009) – see also Chapter 2 where the benefits of NLP are discussed.

They should not imagine a specific job at this stage; they are just getting a sense of the sort of thing they want to do and what it will be like doing it.

Visioning step by step

1 Check in with your client, establish rapport.
2 Explain that this is a process to help them identify and feel really excited about what they want to do in the future. It will also be something they can constantly tap into, to keep themselves motivated and focused on what they want. Tell them that it may be rather different to the goal setting or coaching they have experienced before. Tell them about the power of the unconscious mind.
3 Help your client to relax – e.g. deep breaths in and out, close their eyes, focus on parts of the body from feet up to head, tensing and releasing muscles. If they already practice mindfulness (Hanh, 1975), trance or hypnosis (Gilligan, 1999; Erickson and Rossi, 1992) or meditation (Dharma, 2005), they will be familiar with this kind of technique and find this relatively easy.
4 Talk the client through the visioning: closing your eyes, imagine your working life in five years' time [or whatever is an appropriate length of time for this particular client to imagine].

5 What is happening in your mental image? Get them to describe as vividly as possible, asking supplementary questions as appropriate, e.g.

a Where are you working? Is it an office, or outdoors? Describe it – where is it, what are the surroundings?
b What are you doing? Sitting, standing, etc.?
c Who is there? Add anyone else you'd like to see there
d What colors are there?
e How bright is your image? Make it brighter
f How big is it? Make it bigger
g How far away is it? Bring it nearer
h What sounds can you hear? Make them louder
i What are you feeling? Make that feeling stronger . . . and stronger
j Hold that image and feeling, keep it as bold and vivid as you can.

6 Open your eyes, stand up and 'shake it off', move around, come back to your original position.
7 Bring back your image – with all your senses. Do this several times if necessary.
8 Now you can imagine this whenever you want to motivate yourself towards your chosen career.

Top tips for success

- Develop strong rapport, gain the client's trust, help them relax.
- Use a soft, rhythmic, even tone of voice with little variation. Be aware though that this is a hypnotic tone and could take a client into trance. Unless you are experienced in using hypnotism and trance keep your client above the level of deep trance by occasional variations in tone or questions, e.g. by asking how they are doing. (If you have never been hypnotized and don't know what a hypnotic tone sounds like you will probably have heard people use it unintentionally – and will have called it boring!)
- Ask questions and supplementary questions, following the client's direction.

What's the challenge?

- Client can't vision – no picture comes: get them first to imagine something enjoyable they did recently, experience it again with all their senses
- Client doesn't want to vision – thinks it's too 'pink and fluffy', too 'wacky': talk to them about how and why it works, demonstrate with the exercise above or leave this until you have developed a stronger relationship with the client
- You feel embarrassed about doing this: get comfortable by co-coaching with another coach or practicing with a friend or relative
- If you consider this really is inappropriate for any reason just ask the client questions about their vision in a logical way as a starting point which you may be able to build on later.

Pros

- Very powerful in establishing what a client really wants
- Creates something motivating and tangible for the client to aspire to
- An emotional connection with their desired career is far stronger and more motivating than pure logic.

Cons

- Difficult to use in corporate context or with highly logical clients
- Requires high degree of trust and rapport.

Step 2: Career satisfaction drivers

Figure 4.3 Career decision steps – satisfaction drivers

The second building block, or this may be the first, depending on the client, is to help them discover their career satisfaction drivers – i.e. what motivates them, what is it about a job that makes them enjoy it or dislike it? I often use this first as it is very practical and can be a good, non-threatening way of establishing your relationship with your client – it's pretty 'left–brained' (structured and logical) and produces very quick, almost miraculous, results.

What it is

This is the tool Ursula is talking about at the start of this chapter – it is beautifully simple and in a very short time you can help your client discover the things which motivate them in a job, beyond the actual content, i.e. not whether they wish to be an airline pilot or a nurse but whether they like, for instance, to be in control, to solve problems, or excitement and variety. This will open up a whole range of jobs which they would take pleasure from and also reveal why they may enjoy or not enjoy jobs which, on the face of it, appear to be the same. Most people have between three and six career drivers, usually five.

What is it useful for?

I first worked with this as an internal consultant in a global blue-chip company – career coaching was part of my role as an Organization Development consultant. A colleague and I used it to help managers and professionals who had been identified as talent for the future to understand their career drivers and help them make good, fulfilling career choices which would keep them with the company. I have also used it successfully over the years as an independent coach in many contexts, e.g. for those who are unhappy in their role and unsure why or of what to do next, also people thinking about their next career move. I have found it particularly useful where a client has a pattern of changing jobs frequently as this can reveal to them why they have developed this and help them make better choices in future.

You may wonder, why not just use some sort of questionnaire to find this out? Indeed many career coaches do just that. The power of using this particular technique as a coach is the interaction between the two of you and all the information uncovered through your questioning, much of which was only in their unconscious mind. It gives you the opportunity to pick up things which may not come out when just completing a questionnaire. It is frequently the source of deeper issues the client may need to address to achieve what they want and by noticing these and drawing them to the client's attention they can be the catalyst for subsequent coaching. You are adding value as a coach in a deeper and more holistic way, rather than just presenting them with a questionnaire and analyzing it afterwards.

Overview

Use the proforma (Figure 4.4) to plot a graph showing the client's degree of satisfaction with roles they have held over the last five years or their last five to seven jobs, working from left to right to the present day. They can plot this themselves with your guidance. Use a separate piece of paper to record the responses to your questions.

Through your questioning you will discover what they find motivating and demotivating and you will be able to

Last approx 5 years or 5–7 jobs

Figure 4.4 Career satisfaction drivers graph

draw out the themes that are key for them. They can then use these to inform their career choices. There is no set 'list' of motivators or drivers as there are with other tools (see below). The beauty of this is that it is specific to the individual client. You can use their concepts and their words so they feel real relevance and ownership.

Career satisfaction drivers step by step

1 Have an A4 sized copy of the career satisfaction drivers graph and blank paper to write on. You should take notes and they can draw their own graph.
2 Tell the client the purpose of this and what it will give them, as explained at the start of this section.
3 Ask them to think of their last five or so jobs or the jobs they have had over approximately the last five years – you need enough different roles to be able to bring out the themes.
4 Starting with the first job ask them to put a number, plus or minus, on their degree of satisfaction with that job. They may say that the number changes over time, e.g. they may have liked it a lot at the start but hated it at the end. Plot this on the graph and find out what caused the change.
5 Ask them what they liked/disliked about it that has prompted them to give that score, so that you get a picture of the sort of things they liked or disliked. Ask them what made them decide to move on to their next job – their reasons may be conscious or unconscious so you may need to ask follow up-questions and use your intuition to pick up on what is important. Reflect back to them the reasons they have given.
6 Do the same for the next and subsequent jobs, drawing the graph and making notes. Keeping an open mind as you go along, by the end you will be able to spot common themes that represent their career drivers.
7 Review your notes, telling the client what you believe are their career drivers, giving examples of what they said to support your suggestions. Ask for their thoughts and adjust as necessary to ensure that these are reflected accurately so that these career drivers ring true for them.

8 Talk about their priorities – ask them to rank the most important if they can.

9 Ask them to rate each driver in their current role whether satisfied/dissatisfied or a scale of 1 to 10.

10 Go on to discuss with the client the significance of what they have discovered.

11 After the meeting write up the graph and career drivers and send to your client.

Top tips for success

- Ask questions and follow-up questions for discovery
- Question, listen and write at the same time!
- Look for and draw out themes
- When you are new to this you can use two sessions – use the first one to question and draw the graph then review your notes outside the meeting to identify the drivers which you can then discuss at your next session
- If you have little knowledge of job satisfaction and motivation develop this by studying models such as those mentioned below.

The graph provides a useful visual which in itself can be surprising to clients and reveal things to them that they were not conscious of before, e.g. the stark differences in their level of happiness and unhappiness in different jobs, or how much the level changed over time in a particular role. Your questions and observations make them aware of this as well and the graph helps by showing the full picture at a glance as well as calibration.

You may also find that clients have conflicting drivers or that it's only one or two of their drivers that they are currently unhappy with – for instance, two of my own drivers are work–life balance and worthwhile/meaning. Sometimes this has meant that I have got so involved in my work because I think it's important and valuable that my work–life balance has suffered, not to say I have been completely stressed out! This knowledge has helped me to keep a better balance because I know that achieving a 10 in terms of satisfaction on both those things is not possible and I was searching for a holy grail that doesn't exist!

Case study: Ursula

Ursula hated her job, she felt stressed and unappreciated but didn't fully understand why or what she wanted to do instead. I worked through the career satisfaction drivers graph with her. We identified her drivers and she also rated her satisfaction with each in her current role as it stood:

1 Being part of a team, being in it together – dissatisfied
2 Producing tangible results – partly satisfied
3 Control – dissatisfied
4 Being a trusted expert – dissatisfied
5 Recognition – tangible and intangible – partly satisfied
6 Work–life balance – satisfied.

This demonstrated very clearly why she was dissatisfied with the current situation. We talked about her options and she felt that she needed to get more experience in her specialism before she could look for another job elsewhere that would give her the responsibility, recognition and control she craved. She also realized that in many ways she liked working in her present company and if she could restore the levels of satisfaction she had enjoyed previously she would be very happy to continue working there.

She therefore decided to stay in her current job and make the most of some development opportunities which were about to come her way. This would give her the opportunity to see whether things could be turned around and, if not, she would have some additional skills to enable her to get a job elsewhere.

Shortly after this a new manager became her boss, who took a much more collaborative approach in working with Ursula. She fully appreciated what Ursula was good at and gave her even more development opportunities than those already planned. She also treated her in a far more adult way, rather than having a parent–child relationship as her former manager had.

Thus many of Ursula's satisfaction drivers were restored, her enthusiasm returned and she felt far more positive about her future, either with her current employer or for other possibilities in future.

The long-term benefits of knowing your career drivers became even more apparent when Ursula came to me about 18 months later saying she was being headhunted for an exciting role which would use all the skills and knowledge she'd developed recently but that she didn't know what to do. I got her to go back to her drivers and rate the new role against this – it scored highly on all but work–life balance because it was the other side of the country and would mean her leaving behind the friends and social life she'd taken years to build up. So her decision making was really simplified – she just needed to ask herself whether the other benefits outweighed this and whether anything could be changed in the new role to overcome her reservations. She asked if it would be possible for her to work from home two days a week and go into the office for three. They said no so she decided not to take the new role.

It's incredible the power this tool gives an individual – they can cut through their confusion, take control of their own decision making, negotiate a better deal. They are also able to explain their choice to themselves and others and avoid mistakes because they are tapping into what's most important for them.

Case study: Michael

Michael came to me because he was about to join a new company for a role that was effectively a promotion but he was feeling very distressed and not sure if this was just a natural change curve or whether he was making a huge mistake. Through my questioning he realized he was looking to change his job because he felt his psychological contract, his trust and expectations (Wellin, 2007), with his current employer had been broken – he started to beat himself up, saying that he'd made his decision on an emotional basis, not a logical one. When we looked at his career satisfaction drivers he had a strong driver for meaning and purpose and his contribution had not been recognized by them making him feel undervalued. We looked at his other career satisfaction drivers (he had completed a number of these instruments in the past including the Birkman Method® mentioned below) and he realized that his other drivers were actually still being met. He also felt better when I pointed out that what he had actually done in making his decision (and in making some past career choices) was to get this driver out of kilter with the rest and if he'd simply looked at the others he could have taken a more balanced view.

Once you are aware of them, career satisfaction drivers can be hugely useful at many points in a career. This conversation enabled him to go back to his current employer, who had been keen to retain him, and try to negotiate a deal that would satisfy them both. However, the negotiations didn't go well and there was still a conflict in the psychological contract so he decided to take the new job. He was able to do so at that point from a quite different position, 'positive, professional and empowered'.

An example of career drivers

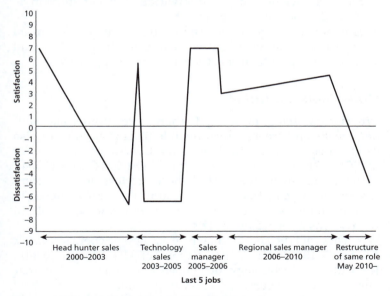

Figure 4.5 **Example of career satisfaction graph**

Figure 4.5 shows Ursula's career satisfaction graph and these are my own career satisfaction drivers:

1 To work with a good boss/colleagues
2 Good work/life balance

3 Learning opportunities
4 Worthwhile with meaning for me
5 Variety.

Pros

- Very quick and powerful to use
- Gives personalized career drivers, unrestricted by a model or formula
- Provides rich information for follow-up coaching.

Cons

- Challenging to question, write, think and categorize as you go
- Some knowledge of job motivation and satisfaction is needed to be able to pick out themes
- A client starting out on their career will have limited experiences to review but you can use school, college and temporary jobs to at least start to create a picture.

Other tools available

Proprietary tools exist and there are numerous self-help books on careers which include tools that you can also use as a coach, e.g. John Lees' *Take Control of Your Career* (2006), or Dave Francis's *Managing Your Own Career* (1994). Although my own view is that these are less effective than the career satisfaction drivers graph, they may appeal to clients who have a need for more research and rigor behind the reasons a technique works.

One of the best known is Edgar Schein's *Career Anchors* (1990). Dr Edgar Schein of the Massachusetts Institute of Technology developed the concept of career anchors from research he carried out among Sloan School graduates. He identified eight anchors which relate to a person's values and can be used to help individuals make career choices which fit with who they truly are. He defined a career anchor as a combination of perceived areas of competence, motives and values which you would preserve at all costs.

His eight anchors are: Technical/functional competence, Managerial competence, Autonomy/independence, Security/ stability, Entrepreneurial creativity, Service/dedication to a cause, Pure challenge, and Lifestyle. Career Anchors online is available at http://www.careeranchorsonline.com/SCA/ startPage.do

Step 3: Values

What are values?

In very simple terms, values are what's important to us and explain why we do what we do; they are what we would not give up in even the most extreme of circumstances. We all have them although many people have never thought about theirs consciously and would not be able to state what their values are. Examples are family, honesty, trustworthiness, loyalty, status, tradition, helping others, discipline, and challenge (O'Connor and Lages, 2004).

Why are they important?

They are important because they inform the choices we make and if an organization or role clashes with our values we will feel very uncomfortable working there or in that position. Because values are often held unconsciously clients may have a bad feeling about something but not know why. Most companies have formally declared values as part of their brand (Mitterer and Brice, 2007) and what actually happens in that organization may or may not be consistent with them. Some values are very obvious and likely to be explicit, such as being environmentally friendly, others less so, e.g. profit before people (CIPD and YouGov, 2010). It's important therefore to help your client uncover their values and those of any organization or role they are thinking of

Figure 4.6 Career decision steps – values

pursuing so that they can choose a career that fits with them. If there is not a good match they will not thrive in that environment.

Values also inform our behavior and attitudes, again often unconsciously, and it's important for clients to understand the impact they can have as this may be positive or negative in the context of the role they desire – see the case study below.

Some values are also a hangover from childhood and early influencers such as parents. They may or may not actually be values the individual has developed themselves and they can sometimes be unhelpful to them – again see the case study below.

Case study

I was coaching a client who had recently been promoted and wanted to improve her relationship with her team. I decided to use the Logical Levels developed by Bateson (1972) and Dilts (1990) to help her find the situations where her relationships were most productive so that she could 'map across' into the one with her team.

Listening to her talk I became aware that she respected people according to their level of education and intelligence and was unconsciously judging people and their worth according to this value from the moment she met them. This was causing her to come across as judgmental and distant to her staff who were not as highly educated and professionally qualified as her.

Just drawing her attention to this made a huge difference, a 'light bulb moment', and I coached her to find shared values which would help her regard her team members as worthwhile and competent. These included a strong sense of ethics and community purpose. She and her team now have a much easier relationship and work together far more productively.

Values: Method

A very simple way to uncover a client's values is with a series of questions which can be used in a variety of ways – you can use it in a coaching session or you can give it to them to work on outside the sessions, preferably with a friend, family member or colleague. The best use of coaching time is for the client to do this outside the session and bring it in for discussion and follow-up coaching.

Questions

- What is most important to you?
- What makes you happy?
- What makes you uncomfortable/unhappy?
- What will you *not* compromise?

The client can also ask others what values they have noticed in them, or you may give observations as their coach.

If they struggle with this you could give them a list of examples to stimulate their thinking. They can either use them as a catalyst to their thinking or pick out four to six as a starting point. They could also pick the four to six which have least meaning for them.

Here is a list you could use:

achievement	happiness	punctuality
adventure	harmony	reliability
challenge	honesty	respect for others
change	independence	responsibility
collaboration	innovation	results-oriented
creativity	integrity	safety
decisiveness	intelligence	security
discipline	joy	service to others
discovery	knowledge	skill
efficiency	leadership	solving problems
energy	loyalty	speed
excellence	merit	spirituality
fairness	money	status
family	openness	structure
freedom	organization	teamwork
friendship	perfection	tolerance
fun	personal growth	tradition
generosity	power	trust
gratitude	practicality	variety
hard work	progress	well-being

In the same way as career satisfaction drivers, this is also likely to give insights into their current or past roles and organizations they have either enjoyed or disliked.

Job and career choice

By this point the client should have enough of a sense of the characteristics of the role that would really suit them that they can either research a specific job or a small range of jobs.

Where a coach adds value in this is by helping them with the process of choosing rather than providing them directly with answers. You are helping them to gain insights, to develop options and make choices. You may assist by helping them identify how to make such choices, including your knowledge of sources of information. Research about specific jobs is something they can do for themselves outside the coaching sessions, using their own network or other resources.

Good sources of information are: their own network, your network, the internet (careers sites such as careers portal, and job search websites such as Change Board or Monster), company websites and careers books. There is more on this in the following chapters.

A good question to ask when someone is unsure whether to take the risk and change is 'Do you still want to be doing this in five or ten years' time/when you retire?' That was certainly one of my own motivations to set up my business; I did not want to still be in corporate life when I retired and that was getting frighteningly close!

Chapter 5 covers this in detail.

Step 4: Well Formed Outcome

To borrow from Milton Erickson (Erickson and Rossi, 1992), if a goal doesn't have a date on it it's just a dream; it's never going to become a reality. So now you have helped your client to expand their thinking and then narrow their choice it's time to frame it in a vivid way which will help them achieve it, including putting a timescale on it.

Figure 4.7 Career decision steps – well formed outcome

The most powerful way to do this is to work with them to set a Well Formed Outcome (WFO). WFO is a concept from NLP (Dilts, Grinder, Bandler and DeLozier, 1989) and it goes way beyond the limitations of traditional goal or objective setting, which generally does not help the individual's motivation or check how congruent the goal is with other aspects of the person's life and work.

Whilst it is best to have a specific role in mind by the time they come to work on the WFO, it is not essential as they can narrow it down as part of this exercise and the actions they take away from it.

What is a WFO?

This is the end result you are looking for – '. . . a desired state, something you don't have in your current state. NLP outcomes . . . have been carefully considered and meet certain conditions that make them realistic, motivating and achievable' (O'Connor, 2001)

How different 'realistic, motivating and achievable' sounds and feels to 'Specific, Measurable and Time-bound' as in the SMART acronym often used in objective setting!

Also objectives are often set around the problem you want to get away from, solve or avoid.

Why does it work?

By using the WFO technique you will give your client the opportunity to consider everything that is going to go into achieving what they want in their career. It fits very well with the work you will already have done with them, enabling them to stay connected with it in a way that's congruent with who they are. In my experience, talking about goals and objectives often takes the client right back into the logical and possibly stressful world of business that you've been helping them to free themselves from for the periods of your coaching so that they can connect with their unconscious and true desires and self. Notice what is happening inside *you* when you read or say the word 'goal' or 'objective' – for me I feel a slight tightening in my chest and start to think of acronyms such as SMART and the pressure of managerial and organizational expectations to achieve.

It may not be quite like that for you or your client but I believe framing what the client wants in a way that is different takes it away from the context of the often pressurized world of everyday business and what they want to change or get away from, and creates curiosity and a freer way of thinking for them. It also enables them to think more broadly about what they want and how they will get it.

A WFO is based on 'outcome' rather than 'problem' thinking. The mind is actually very, very good at giving you what you put your attention on and so if your client focuses on their career problems and what they don't want, that is what they will get (Knight, 1999). To use a simple example, if you ride a bike and you've ever thought, 'don't hit that kerb' or 'mind those stinging nettles', or if you play golf and have thought, 'mind that tree/bunker/lake', what happens? You find yourself tangled up with the thing you are thinking of! If I say to you 'Don't think of a pink giraffe with blue spots' what do you immediately think of? Change your thoughts to 'keep to the center of the track', 'hit the ball straight down the fairway', and that is what you will do. Similarly, in the world of work, if you are thinking about what you want to get away from in your current job or are worrying about doing or saying the wrong thing those are the things you will focus on and be stuck with.

It also tests whether the client really does want what they think they want, helps them think through the wider implications of achieving it and starts to uncover things which may stop or impede them.

Well Formed Outcome (WFO): Method

In summary

This involves you taking the client through a series of questions to develop a clearer idea of what they want to achieve and how they are going to do it. They will develop success measures, understand the full impact of their outcome, whether the price is worth paying and will identify the resources they have or need to be successful. Finally you will help them decide what action to take, in particular the first action they can take to make the biggest step toward getting the outcome they want.

There are many versions of the method for setting a WFO, e.g. in Sue Knight's *NLP at Work* (2009) and Joseph O'Connor's *NLP Workbook* (2001) and *Coaching with NLP* (O'Connor and Lages, 2004). This is my version and you can adapt it to suit you and your individual clients.

In detail

You are going to ask your client a series of questions to help them work through what they want and how they are going to get it, and test whether they really do want it! You should take notes for the client, using their own words as far as possible.

1 *What do you really want?* This should be expressed in the positive. You may need to ask the question several times or ask supplementary questions to help your client, especially if they are very accustomed to 'problem' thinking. For instance, 'so if you don't want . . ., what would you like instead?' (Lawley and Tompkins, 2000).

Once the client has defined what they want ask them how they would like you to refer to it, e.g. to be a teacher, be an authentic and inspirational manager, work in a company which enhances the environment. After this use the words they choose whenever you refer to their WFO as this will give them ownership and start to make it real for them. Also refer to it in the present tense and as an identity if possible, as if they already have achieved it e.g. 'what does being a teacher look like, feel like?' and so on.

2 *How will you know when you have succeeded?* This again is an opportunity to bring to life what the client wants, to get them connected to it and experience what it would be like. What they are looking for is evidence that will demonstrate that they have succeeded. Help them to imagine what it will be like by asking questions which tap into all their senses, e.g.

- What does it look like? What do you see around you? Who else is there? Where are you?
- What does it sound like? What do you hear? What are you saying? What are those around you saying?
- What does it feel like? What are you feeling? Where is that feeling in your body? How strong is it?
- What is it like having succeeded? Help them to develop a metaphor which they can use as a 'shorthand', e.g. 'it's like surfing – it feels exciting and slightly dangerous as well!' They could even find or draw a picture which they can carry with them to remind them. We all live by metaphors, and noticing and exploring them can be extremely powerful and is the essence of 'Clean Language'. There is more on this in Chapter 2 (Lakoff and Johnson, 1980; Sullivan and Rees, 2008).

This may well have been covered in a visioning session so you may just need to reflect back on that at this stage.

3 *Where, when and with whom do you want this?* They may already have answered the 'Where' and 'With Whom' elements, but if not ensure these are clear, e.g. they may have established that they want to be a manager and you may help them explore here what type of company that would be with.

Get them to commit to a timescale at this point.

4 *What resources do you have that will help you?* Help them discover what they need:

- tangible objects, e.g. computer, car, home office, finances
- other people, e.g. family, friends, colleagues, mentor, coach, role models, networks

- personal, e.g. skills, capabilities, personality, knowledge, health and fitness, values.

Ask questions to explore which resources they already have and those they would need to develop or acquire in order to achieve their WFO.

Important questions to ask are:

- How much of your outcome is within your own control? What can you do yourself to achieve it? It is essential to ensure that it is something they can do themselves and not something where they are reliant on others
- Who else can help you? How can you motivate them to help you, i.e. what can you offer that will help *them*?
- Who do you need to influence? How can you do that?

5 *What are the wider consequences of achieving this?*

- Who else will be affected and how? Will they see what you want as positive or negative? e.g. spouse, children, parents, your team
- What will it take from you? e.g. time and effort to achieve and maintain it, risk taking, discomfort
- What will you have to give up? These may be superficial things such as 'going to the pub in the evening' but they could be very profound things such as limiting or other beliefs and may not be immediately evident. Often this will need to be picked up in later coaching sessions
- What is good about the present situation? What do you want to keep? This may also reveal benefits the client was not conscious of which have actually been keeping them in the place they are. For instance, they know more about the job than anyone else and are worried about knowing very little in a new role
- What might be the unintended consequences?
- Are you willing to pay the price? This may be financial or have nothing to do with money.

6 *Is your outcome in keeping with who you are?*

- Does it fit with your values?
- Does it fit with your identity? If it doesn't fit with the client's current identity this will be something to work

on in a future coaching session. To be successful in achieving any outcome it must be consistent with how they see themselves and who they are.

7 *Is this outcome manageable and motivating? How committed to it are you?* If the outcome is too big to think about and manage in one go help the coachee to break it down into more manageable chunks and set outcomes for these. For instance, if they want to be a lawyer and need to get a qualification first, think initially about this.

Ask how motivated they are to achieve this – it may be helpful to calibrate this, e.g. ask them how motivated they are on a scale of 1 to 10. What number will it need to be for them to put in the necessary commitment and work, especially when the going gets tough? It's really worth spending some time on this.

8 *Action*

   – What is the first thing you could do that will make the biggest difference?
   – What are the other things you will do to achieve this?
   – What are the barriers you will need to overcome?

9 *How will you know you are on track?* Ask similar questions to question 2 so that they can find evidence to show whether they are on or off track to achieving what they want. For example if they are going to study, what will be happening at the end of the first term?

You may well find that there are gaps in what the client knows at this point. Chapter 5 provides approaches and tools which will go to the next level of detail and fill those holes.

Top tips for success

* Listen deeply to what the client is saying, i.e. don't just accept everything they say at face value, understand the significance
* Use your intuition to follow leads into areas that may give the client new insights and to decide whether to

follow those in the moment or to make a 'note to self' to explore them at another time.

What's the challenge?

- Asking insightful questions, listening deeply and taking notes at the same time! Practice, practice, practice
- Knowing which leads to follow and when – again practice and use your intuition.

Case study

Back in 2006 I decided I wanted to learn about NLP and signed up for Sue Knight's NLP Business Practitioner course. Unfortunately I was ill at the time of the final workshop and assessment and wasn't able to complete my qualification with the people I'd got to know and worked so personally and profoundly with over several months. I knew I wanted to complete the course but felt unsure about how to and kept procrastinating and talking myself out of all the options I came up with.

Eventually I decided to use one of Sue's first principles of NLP and 'apply to self' – I decided to set a Well Formed Outcome. Starting to think about what I really wanted I realized that I wanted not only to get my qualification but also to be an assistant on one of Sue's courses. I felt so excited at that prospect – and so brave! – I rang Sue immediately and put my proposal to her that I should come to one of her introductory courses, complete my assessment and act as one of her assistants. She immediately said yes!

The amazing thing was not only that I achieved something which had been a desire I'd buried in my unconscious mind but how quickly and easily I achieved it, beating the timescale I'd set myself by miles!

Pros

- Connects the client with what they want in both a logical and emotional way – shows them both what and how

- Uncovers matters in the unconscious which will impact the client's ability to achieve what they want which can be addressed in later coaching sessions
- Can be used effectively by an inexperienced coach and can be very profound in the hands of someone highly skilled.

Cons

- May be uncomfortable for those with very logical, left-brained modes of thinking preferences
- Can take a long time to work through all the questions thoroughly – but the client can do more work on it outside the coaching session.

More possibilities

Clean Language

Clean Language (see Chapter 2) can be very powerful here, especially the two 'foundation' questions: 'Is there anything else about . . .' and 'What kind of . . . is that . . .' (Tompkins and Lawley, 2000).

Developing their Well Formed Outcome may have identified aspects which it may be helpful for the client to follow up either with you or independently or with other help, perhaps from their HR Department. For example:

Logical Levels

This is covered in more depth in Chapter 2. In helping your client with their career choice you can use it to check that all they have decided is congruent and to give you cues as to areas for exploration in further coaching sessions.

Strengths finder

Use Buckingham and Clifton's *Now Discover Your Strengths* (2005) or Rath's *Strengths Finder 2.0* (2007). You can purchase these online or at any good bookshop, and can also access an online questionnaire which produces a report of personal strengths.

The strengths-based approach is very affirming, especially for those whose self-esteem and confidence is low and who are accustomed to 'deficit focused' performance management systems.

360-degree feedback

Your client could gather feedback on their strengths and capabilities from peers, direct reports, customers and so on to give them a better understanding of their strengths and development needs. This can be done formally, including using an online tool, many of which are available commercially and are often used by businesses as part of management development. Your client may be able to access one through their HR manager. Alternatively they or you can do this informally by talking to colleagues and asking about particular capabilities they want to understand others' perspectives on.

There may be a cost to the client and/or organizations for using 360-degree feedback and a number of organizations provide a service which can be tailored.

Explaining and discussing 360-degree feedback reports is something I am often asked to do by organizations I work with and this is a useful service to offer as a Career Transition coach.

Psychometrics and personality surveys

Many tools are available to help clients understand their preferences and strengths in areas which can help inform them about careers which would be right for them or give personal insights when transitioning into a new role. Some of these are quite expensive, very detailed and require a fully qualified facilitator to administer and interpret them – shortened versions of some are available online to give a taster.

Some examples are:

- Birkman Method®: http://www.birkman.com/birkman Method/whatIsTheBirkmanMethod.php

- Myers-Briggs Type Indicator® (MBTI®): http://www. myersbriggs.org/
- Herrmann Brain Dominance Instrument® (HBDI®): http:// www.hbdi.com/
- SHL's Occupational Personality Questionnaire (OPQ32r): http://www.shl.com/WhatWeDo/PersonalityAssessment/ Pages/OPQQuestionnaire.aspx
- 16 PF® (16 personality factors): http://www.pearson assessments.com/HAIWEB/Cultures/en-us/Product detail.htm?Pid=PAg101&Mode=summary
- DiSC (Dominance, Influence, Steadiness, Conscientiousness): DiSC® is a trademark of the US Inscape Publishing company: http://www.inscapepublishing.com/. Other versions of DiSC profiling are available through other suppliers.

As a Career Transition coach you may find it useful to become qualified to use some of these but in my experience it is not essential, and may not be a good return on your investment of time and money. Many organizations provide training in psychometrics, e.g. OPP (see www.opp.com/en/ training).

Wheel of Life

This is a very well-known coaching tool which can be used in career transitions, for example, helping the client to identify what is important in their life and how satisfied they are with the different aspects. There are numerous versions and the client can choose headings which are important to them.

Start by asking the client to choose about eight areas of their life in which they want to be satisfied – use the example wheel in Figure 4.8 as a guide. Then ask them to plot how satisfied they are currently with each aspect by marking a score between zero and ten with a cross on the appropriate radius. Join the crosses to see how balanced their life is currently – the wheel may make a very uncomfortable ride! They can then plot the scores they would like to have and use the 'gap' as the basis for deciding where their priority actions lie. In the spaces they can write their goals/activities for each area.

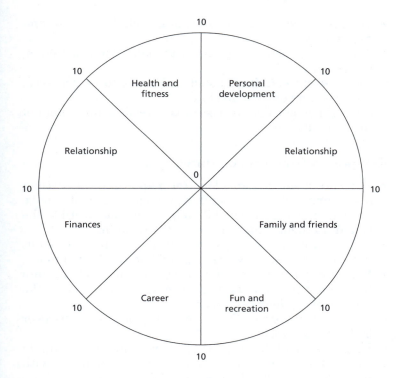

Figure 4.8 **Wheel of life**

This again is a good starting point for discussion and coaching, helping them see where they are satisfied and dissatisfied and what they would need to do to achieve a better balance.

Career development plan

Below are some headings you can put into a proforma which your client could use to pull together their plan in a more formal way and monitor their progress.

- My *ultimate outcome* including date to be completed and actually achieved

- *Success milestones* with dates for completion, review and date achieved
- *Action plan:* actions agreed with dates for completion, review and achieved
- *Development activities:* listed and dates to be achieved, reviewed and date completed
- *Success log:* journal all successes towards achievement of the ultimate outcome.

Key points from this chapter

- Get your client to take a long-term approach rather than just trying to fix an immediate problem – the tools I have recommended here should help in demonstrating the benefit to them if they are reluctant to do so.
- Help your client develop a vivid vision of what they want in their career so they are inspired and committed to it.
- Find any patterns in their career to date and tap into their conscious and unconscious mind to help them make full use of all their resources.
- Use the Well Formed Outcome (WFO) process to discover both what and how.
- Help the client to 'test' what they think they want to ensure they want it badly enough and that it fits with their identity and enhances their life.

5

Getting there

I recall when I was an HR Business Partner, one candidate who had been serially unsuccessful in getting promoted was feeling very frustrated: 'We all know it's a game. We just don't know what the rules are!' This chapter is the point where you steer your coachee through the 'rules of the game' of recruitment, promotion and setting up their own business.

In Chapter 4 you looked at the big picture, now your client is going to get down to the nitty-gritty, the practical work that will help them achieve what they want. You have reached Stage 2 of the career transition journey: *Preparation and search: CV and interview preparation, networking, personal branding and 'pitching', confidence and self-belief.*

This stage of career transition coaching requires a rather different approach as a coach and parts of it are more akin to mentoring than content-free coaching; many clients are looking for information so you need to be able to contribute both process and content during this phase – to quote Julie Blunt in her article 'The Art of Work' (2011), it's not a content-free zone!

Beware the bear trap though – although you are providing information, knowledge, guidance and options for your client you should still not be telling them what to do and taking the responsibility for their decisions upon yourself, as with any coaching.

This chapter provides approaches to satisfy those practical needs whilst achieving that balance. It looks in depth at the two most common options of:

1 finding a new role – whether it be promotion or change of role or career inside or outside the same organization
2 self-employment – which includes freelancing, contracting or working as an associate

and how you can support your client in making them a reality. It also considers the transition to retirement.

That said, the same principles apply to both and the same coaching approaches will help in both cases. Whether your client wants to be employed or self-employed you need to help them consider:

1 *Self-assessment:* what are the skills and qualities they have or need to develop for their chosen option?
2 *Opportunity assessment:* what does the market need, and how do they and their ideas measure up?
3 *Branding:* self, and business if self-employed. What is their Unique Selling Point (USP)? How do they want to be seen? This includes their CV or personal profile as well as their business identity for the self-employed.
4 *Marketing:* how and where are they going to market themselves? The critical importance of networking and online presence.
5 *Selling:* how will they sell themselves and their products or services? Preparing a CV, covering letter, personal profile or business proposal.
6 *Negotiation and decision making:* which job to take, negotiating an employment package, what fees or product prices to charge and how to negotiate them, which business structure to adopt or accountant to use.

Here is a summary of some useful approaches and tools you can use at each of these stages:

Issue	Approaches
Self-assessment	SWOT, psychometrics e.g. motivational maps, Insights, self-assessment questionnaire, Logical Levels
Opportunity assessment	SWOT, skills audit
Branding	Logical Levels
Marketing	CV, cover note, feedback
Selling	Interview prep and practice – STAR technique, feedback. Visualization, anchoring to a positive feeling and Cognitive Behavioral Coaching (CBC)
Negotiation and decision making	Gestalt, convincer patterns, Kahneman anchoring, share and create stories
Any and every stage	Insightful questions

Figure 5.1 Getting there – approaches and tools

Employment: Finding a new role

We will look at:

- What the market is demanding in the client's chosen role and how do they currently match up to it – that is, their 'employability' and what they need to do to increase it
- Preparation for their career campaign e.g. CV preparation
- Conducting the campaign – where and how to look, interview preparation, etc.
- Decision making, including salary and employment package negotiation.

I will cover the principles and essentials here but there is no substitute for your own knowledge and experience and you do need to be a 'subject matter expert' on the job market – not on every job or sector but on how the market works and 'what the rules of the game are'.

Employability

Anyone wanting to participate in the world of work needs to think about their own 'employability', which the CBI (2007) has defined as 'A set of attributes, skills and knowledge that all labor market participants should possess to ensure they have the capability of being effective in the workplace – to the benefit of themselves, their employer and the wider economy.' The CBI includes self-management, team working, business and customer awareness, problem solving, communication and literacy, application of numeracy, application of information technology, positive attitude and entrepreneurship/enterprise. This '101' of employability applies no matter what stage of their career a person is at, whether just starting out as a fresh-faced graduate (as in the case of the CBI report) or having been in the job market for years. Deni Lyall of Winning Performance says that, from her experience of outplacement coaching with individuals from top to bottom of organizations, if you have energy you are much more likely to get a job. If you are timid and hold back, then you may need to think about how the recruiter might view that. What the world wants and expects is changing faster than ever before.

So one of the first steps is for your coachee to think about what is needed in the field or role they want to work in. Some exploration may be necessary on their part, for instance internet research, relevant professional bodies or talking to people in their network. Who do they know who can help them? Once they have a clear idea of the skills, knowledge and personal attributes required they are ready to start looking at how they match up and what gaps they need to fill.

A simple and very effective way to explore their employability is to complete a SWOT analysis – Strengths, Weaknesses, Opportunities and Threats.

SWOT (strengths, weaknesses, opportunities, threats)

What it is and why it works

SWOT is frequently used in business so it is a tool that many clients will already be familiar with – what they probably won't have done is used it on themselves. If you have not used it before yourself, it is a simple four-box matrix – Strengths and Weaknesses are aspects which are internal to the client (e.g. skills they have such as being well organized or good at relationship building, or strong values, for instance a high level of integrity) whilst Threats and Opportunities are external to them (e.g. an opportunity may be that a redundancy package is available, providing a financial cushion, whilst a threat could be that the economy is in recession and there are not many jobs on the market). The concept originates from 1960s research at the Stanford Research Institute (Fleisher and Bensoussan, 2002)

How and when to use it

As with so many tools, SWOT works on many different levels and can serve a variety of purposes. It provides a simple framework for a 'stocktake' which can be taken away by the client to complete between sessions and used as the basis for future coaching sessions. It is not onerous and can even be broken down into bite-sized chunks. It is an excellent way of developing self-awareness and stimulating ideas.

So says Karen Williams of Self Discovery Coaching who uses this with most of her career transition clients. She normally sets it as 'homework' after the first or second coaching session, reviewing it at the next. In her experience the beauty of it is that it

- uncovers transferable skills and strengths
- performs a skills audit
- helps with completion of the client's CV
- is a confidence booster – many clients, especially those later in their career who have been in the same role or organization for a long time, don't realize their strengths.

Goal...

Strengths	Weaknesses
What skills and capabilities do you have?	What gaps in your capabilities and skills do you need to develop?
In what areas do you excel?	What personal difficulties do you need to overcome to achieve your goal? (E.g. skills gaps, personal presence, financial reserves)
What qualifications, accreditations, experience or qualities make you unique?	
What do others say are your strengths?	What do others say are your weaknesses?
Opportunities	**Threats**
What opportunities are available to you?	What obstacles are you facing?
Who do you know who could help you achieve success?	What external factors may hinder your success? (E.g. economic conditions, new technologies, legislation)
What external factors are in your favor? (E.g. market developments, partnership opportunities, local employment market)	Who or what might get in your way?

Figure 5.2 **SWOT analysis template**

She agrees the topic to focus on with the client, whether it might be their desire to change jobs or get a promotion, and she urges them to use all the sources of data at their disposal – appraisals, 360 degree surveys, psychometrics, friends and family, etc. It serves as a 'Johari window' (Luft and Ingham, 1955) for clients to reflect on what they already know about themselves, what others know about them and to lead into coaching which can uncover further potential.

An example based on questions Karen includes in her SWOT is shown in Figure 5.2.

Top tips for success

- Strong contracting is important – establish how committed and motivated they are to making a change, which will involve considerable work on their part, including completing the SWOT

- Position it within your process for supporting clients in career transition and make time to explain it face to face, don't email it
- Explain how to use it in the personal context if they have used it in business
- Explore and expand on it; don't just take their initial list, look for possibilities they have not considered
- Put it into a context, i.e. base it around a specific goal
- Use the client's language
- Appreciate that some clients need more help with it than others – Karen provides a set of example questions and criteria, examples of which are shown in Figure 5.2.

What's the challenge?

- Some clients find it very difficult to see their strengths, others their weaknesses
- Some don't like to go into this much detail
- Some don't keep the commitments they make to actions between sessions and fail to complete it
- Some may find it difficult to complete this form without the coach supporting and developing their thought processes.

Pros

- Develops self-awareness
- Simple concept
- Feeds into other things, e.g. interviews, CVs, and issues which can be coached, e.g. confidence, self-awareness.

Cons

- Needs honesty from client, their network and the coach about what they are good at and realism about the external environment
- Some get frustrated with their weaknesses and that can cause a dip in their confidence which needs in-depth coaching
- Some are just resistant to change.

Case study: Penny

Karen was working with Penny who wanted to change careers after working ten years in the same organization in a remote country area. Her relationship with her manager was not good and there were no opportunities for advancement. What had been an exciting, active job in a beautiful environment had now become a bit of a straitjacket and she felt that she should change jobs and industry now before it became more difficult as she got older and had experience in only one area.

As a result of the SWOT Penny found transferable strengths that she could use in other sectors; she established essential content for her CV that focused on where she wanted to get to. It enabled her to identify pros and cons about different job possibilities and a talent for marketing, which had been a part of her role but not actually included in her job description. Without the SWOT and subsequent coaching she would probably never have identified this talent and job possibility.

The outcome was that she had a new and impressive CV, a focus and an idea of the job she wanted, and a career development plan, and so was looking for interview opportunities. She also knew the type of job and organization she did not want, so was not wasting her time being distracted and demoralized by applying for things which were not right for her. In the difficult job climate of this time she also had a plan for what she would do if she had not got her ideal job by a certain date. She was focused and motivated.

It's important to manage clients' expectations, especially in a difficult employment climate – you can help them with strategies which they can carry forward into the rest of their life as well as their career search but they will have to work hard at it and you cannot guarantee them a job by the end of your coaching contract.

Some clients are naturally more inclined to 'away from' thinking and this tendency is likely to be even more apparent in times of high unemployment – job hunters focus on the *lack* of jobs in the market and forget that even with 15 percent unemployment 85 percent of people *do* have jobs. How you get and keep yourself in the 85 percent should be the focus, rather than fear of the 15 percent – you *will* get what you focus on! As Henry Ford is credited with saying, whether you think you can or can't do something, you'll be right. If you think you won't get a job the likelihood is you won't, if you think you will – you will!

The client's next actions will depend on what the SWOT reveals. They may need to put in place a development plan to hone their skills and knowledge or develop their resources such as their network.

Preparation for their job search campaign

This involves creating the profiles and materials for their job search – their CV, covering letter and online profiles. The primary purpose of these is to showcase themselves and get to the next stage of the recruitment process, usually an interview – these are *marketing* documents not just 'information sources'. You can help your client by

- Providing key pointers and a CV format, showing where and how to create an online presence
- Helping them get into the right state to produce their materials
- Critiquing and helping them improve their materials

It's little wonder that many people dread writing a CV or find it intensely confusing – if you search out advice on the subject you will find much of it is conflicting or contradictory. However, there are some universal principles to bear in mind:

- This is their window on the world – it is what they really want people to know about them.
- It should present a compelling picture which encapsulates why the recruiter would want to employ them.
- It should be an authentic reflection of who they are – their personality and achievements should shine through. It may follow a standard format but it should be distinctive.
- It must be accurate and perfectly presented – dates, spelling and grammar correct, well-organized and easy to follow, easy to find relevant information, properly aligned, consistent font.

- It should be succinct and containing only relevant information. Remember the recruiter may be reading hundreds of applications and they are human (well, mostly – many do use automated sifting systems). They get bored easily and are looking for reasons to reject applications.
- Include only achievements and positive qualities, not things that went wrong or things that would be regarded as weaknesses. At this stage the recruiter wants to know what the candidate *can* do – the interview is the place for them to explore the potential downside of employing them.
- Tailor to the job you are applying for – you must do your homework, researching the company and any people mentioned in the advert so that you can tailor to your style and culture. Use the words the advert uses (automated systems often look for precise matches). Include only experience and achievements relevant to the job requirements.

The most important thing

Creating CVs and covering letters that have the desired impact is primarily about mind-set and it's essential that the client gets themselves into a positive state to write. It is a virtuous circle as well – it's really motivating to focus on achievements and positive qualities and present them in a good-looking profile. A really effective way to do this is to use the Logical Levels (Dilts and DeLozier, 2000) – see Chapter 2. Get your client to work through the levels identifying the positive things they have to offer at each and in particular to adopt the identity of the job they are applying for – if they want to be a General Manager that is how they should imagine themselves. They will then write from a confident and positive frame of mind, from the standpoint of a GM.

CV format

Get your coachee to do some research of their own to develop a format that works best for them, for instance, reviewing adverts for the type of role they want to apply for and recommended CV formats. These days it is very easy to do this online by looking at recruitment sites appropriate to their focus. In this way they will find something that is authentic for them, rather than just taking your format. However, this *is* the kind of advice coachees are looking for so you should develop a standard format you can give them as a starting point.

Covering letter

An effective covering letter is essential – this makes clear to the recruiter the 'so what' factor, spelling out why and how they match the criteria and are the best person for the job. It should demonstrate what the person has achieved, what the impact has been and how that meets what the job is calling for.

Start by stating clearly which role they are applying for, including any reference number. I find the best way to construct it is to go through the advert, highlight the key attributes, qualifications and experience and so on that are asked for, then identify what are the most significant examples in your own experience which match up. Also form an overall sense of what the recruiter is looking for that is not mentioned specifically so that the letter can reflect this in the points stressed and the general impression the coachee gives of themselves; are they looking for someone who is hands-on rather than strategic, are they more interested in experience than qualifications?

Finish strongly in a way that invites them to call you for interview: 'By working with me I am confident you will achieve the growth you are looking for and would welcome the opportunity to discuss with you the contribution I could make to Blah Blah plc'.

If there is something the organization is asking for which is missing from what the coachee is offering, what should they do? Look for transferable skills or experience in their CV and stress how those fit the bill.

Conducting the campaign

There are two approaches your coachee should take here, both broad and specific. The first is an overarching one of proactively putting themselves out into the 'market', networking and building their reputation. No one is going to come knocking on their door looking for them, they *have* to be visible and active, even if they are looking within their current organization. This is easier than it has ever been with the availability of the internet and company intranets. The second is more specific: for an external search, to sign up with relevant recruitment agencies, head hunters or websites, to apply for advertised roles or, best of all, to ensure they are considered by or through people in their own network. Many jobs are never advertised – it is definitely not what you know but who you know.

Even for an internal search it's not sufficient to perform well and work hard (Goddard, 2011) although these may be prerequisites. Again, you need to know the 'rules of the game', e.g. who actually makes the decisions and how? How can the coachee get feedback on how they are regarded? Their boss or HR manager may be good sources of information and even influence. The same principles apply as in the open market – how do they get themselves noticed and their talents and achievements recognized? It might be by volunteering for cross-departmental projects or high profile opportunities, ensuring their monthly reports are well thought out and sell what they have done. Again, use their own network and that of those who think highly of them to get introductions to people they may wish to work for – have coffee with them. As one friend of mine said, 'I've met everyone in town who can talk and drink coffee'. Yes, they'll buy an awful lot of coffees! They should keep up with their network on an ongoing basis though so people don't think they only want to meet when they want something! A mentor is also a great way of getting information, advice and introductions. Choose carefully and ensure it *is* someone influential. I remember a colleague telling me that her mentor was the director of my department and how impressed I was. How on earth did she do that? Answer: she asked! Not only was she getting top quality support but also the reflected glow of saying her mentor was a Director – who wouldn't think 'She must be good if a Director is interested in her'?

Networking, reputation building and online applications

Networking and reputation building are vital for career aspirations both inside and outside the current company and can be achieved personally and/or virtually, i.e. online using social media channels. Having an online presence is no longer optional – what is the first thing I do when I meet someone new? An internet search to find out more about them. Establishing your personal brand and telling your own story is vital. This also enables them to keep in touch with what is happening in the job market and build useful contacts.

The Kelly Global Workforce Survey (Kelly Services, 2011a) found that social networks and online methods of finding jobs were frequently used, although the proportions of job seekers using them varied by generation. Gen Y used social networks very actively for job search with 40 percent favoring Facebook, followed by LinkedIn (23 percent). Twenty-four percent of Gen X and Baby Boomers use social networking, primarily LinkedIn, to look for jobs. The good news is that this does not have to be time-consuming – across all generations, approximately two-thirds of respondents spent one hour or less on social media sites each day.

Job seekers can post their profile, connect with people they know and take part in forums and groups which match their interests and expertise – helping others and showcasing their talents. Equally they can, and should, follow companies they are interested in working for, says Gerry O'Neill of Penna. He says there is absolutely no excuse to be unaware of what is going on in any company you might apply for.

The choice of physical or virtual networking and reputation building and the balance between them needs careful consideration, so help your coachee explore their options and narrow it down to the best 'time to impact' ratio for them and their aspirations. They need to 'be' where their potential employers are present, perhaps at meetings of their professional association, on LinkedIn or participating in online discussion forums.

I well remember when I was looking for an interim role and was networking like mad. I was going regularly to a monthly meeting for HR professionals and always asked for the list of attendees for that evening so I knew who I wanted to talk to. To my delight the Director I was going to be interviewed by the very next day was also attending. I was able to ensure that we were in the same discussion group and that I shone in the conversation. Next day I could walk in confidently and say how good it was to see her again and refer back to topics we had discussed. Yes, I did get the job!

I'm not here to sell LinkedIn or provide a detailed description of its benefits. The point is that you, as coach, need to be aware of the social media platforms that are available and their benefits and to help your coachee find and use the ones that will best match their needs and preferences. Their time is limited so you need to help them focus their efforts to get the best return. Once again you are getting them to think broadly about their options and then narrow it down.

When it comes to actually applying for jobs, according to Kelly (2011a) 24 percent of Generation X used online job boards and 22 percent word of mouth to find their current role. For Generation Y the figures were 31 and 23 percent respectively. Even 19 percent of Baby Boomers secured their latest positions through online job boards, with the same proportion through direct approaches from employers and 22 percent by word-of-mouth. One can only think that the use of online methods of recruitment and job search are set to continue and increase – every well-known company has its recruitment page on its website as do newspapers, professional publications and recruitment agencies, be they generalist or specialists in either professions such as law or accountancy, or graduate, blue collar, white collar, senior level; permanent, temporary, contract or interim. It's all there!

Interview preparation

You can help your client prepare to give their best performance on both practical and psychological levels.

Key principles to bear in mind

- The interviewer wants them to do well – believe me, having been on the other side of the fence, there is nothing more demoralizing that sitting through a day or even days of interviews with candidates who are ill-prepared, reticent, unfocused and have no idea how to demonstrate their suitability for the job.
- It's another selling job! Without being arrogant, they should be able to describe their experience and contribution – let this speak for itself rather than just saying how wonderful *they* think they are.
- Time for more homework – learn as much as they can about the company and whoever will be interviewing them. Most of this is possible online, through printed sources and through their own network – who do they know who could help? Networking again!
- They should prepare answers in advance to all the questions they might be asked. For each, know what the three key points are they want to make. In the heat of the moment they may forget some detail but they will be able to ensure they include what's most important if they are well rehearsed. Link things about themselves to what they know about the company, e.g. if applying for a marketing role and the company has a particular campaign going on in the media, talk about how that relates to a similar one they have worked on.
- Equally they should develop questions of their own that they wish to ask the interviewers which demonstrate that they know something about the company. Ensure they are relevant to the role they have applied for but not too narrow and personal, e.g. what the pay and bonus arrangements are. They can ask those when they are offered the job!
- Do answer the question the interviewer asks, not the one they wish they had asked, whilst ensuring that they put across all the key points in favor of themselves as the successful candidate.
- Use the STAR process (see below) to answer questions about experience and achievements – this ensures they cover the most important aspects in a logical and understandable way.

- When they have made all their key points stop, don't just drift on and peter out. . . .
- At the end of the interview do two things – mentally reflect back on whether there is anything they think the interviewer had doubts about in their answers. Say something along the lines of, 'I sensed that you had some concerns about my length of my experience in the legal sector. I want to reassure you that I really understand what is most important, that is, the need to build long-term client relationships whilst also focusing on fee-earning, and I am easily able to transfer all the skills I have learnt in other sectors to your practice. I think I have demonstrated that with my success across all the sectors I have worked in'.
- If there is anything vital they haven't had the chance to mention, say there is something they think it's important for the interviewer to know that they would like to add.
- Sum up why they believe they are the best candidate.
- Mock interviews can be invaluable – offering this as a coach can really help your client. I recall the first time I was on the receiving end of this and what an absolute mess I made of it – I just knew I could *never* be that bad again!

Practical support you can give

This includes giving feedback on their prepared answers to likely questions and interview practice, with you and friends and relatives.

Interview questions. Many companies have highly trained and skilled interviewers and a set process they follow; most are a version or combination of what Salgado and Moscoso (2002) named Structured Behavioral Interviews (SBI). They might be called competency-based, behavioral (BDI – Behavioral Description Interviewing (Janz, 1977, 1982, 1989), to use the formal name), situational (SI – Situational Interviewing (Latham, Saari, Pursell and Campion (1980)) or criteria-based. Others use unstructured or semi-structured interviews and the quality of interviewing varies considerably.

Whoever or whatever approach they are faced with, your client needs to be prepared to be proactive and ensure they include all the key information which makes them the best person for the job, while letting their personality shine through.

Preparation and practice are key and you can help with both. Candidates should prepare descriptions of all their key achievements and significant events, and consider possible pitfalls in their CV and covering letter. Also plan answers to powerful interview questions such as 'Why should I appoint you to this job?' 'How will you add value in 30/60/90 days?' (Mattson, quoted by Levin-Epstein, 2011). A CV is effectively an invitation to an interviewer to ask about those topics and being prepared means the answer will be better and also gives confidence to the candidate.

A fantastic site to help with interview preparation is http://www.jobsite.co.uk/bemyinterviewer/ where you can hear killer interview questions asked by top business people such as Duncan Bannatyne, serial entrepreneur. This is highly recommended by Deni Lyall. Or there is Tony Goddard Consulting's blog which gives a list of the most commonly asked questions, from which you can help your coachee to identify the ones they are most likely to be asked for the job they are being interviewed for: http://www.tonygoddardconsulting.com/career-coaching/interview-questions/. In particular Tony believes they should be able to run through their CV in four minutes in a positive and concise manner.

A company may send a list of competencies to applicants, or candidates may be able to pick out the main ones required from the advert. They can then match their prepared examples to these, developing an answer to demonstrate their achievements in each area. If no list is available or apparent the following will serve as a useful guide:

- Results and performance focus
- Customer focus
- Problem solving and decision making
- Team working
- Communication skills
- Relationship building

- Creativity and innovation
- Leading people
- Financial and commercial
- Strategy and planning
- 'Professional/technical', i.e. related to the specialism of the job.

'STAR' technique. A highly effective approach to use to prepare for and to answer interview questions is the STAR technique. STAR stands for Situation, Task, Action and Results.

This looks at what the candidate has actually done rather than what they say they would do in a given situation, in relation to competencies required to do a particular job successfully.

Once again they should go back to the advert and CV and prepare answers on the key areas the advert asks for – if it asks for someone who is results-orientated, identify the best example from the CV and prepare an answer for that. Read between the lines as well and understand what is important but not actually spelled out. Decide also what you think is important in relation to what you have to offer so that you have a USP, Unique Selling Point. Give strong messages about what it takes to succeed, as per Vivian Giang's interview with Seth Godin, 'If You're An Average Worker, You're Going Straight to the Bottom' (Giang, 2012). Key message: if you differentiate yourself and say what's unique about you, employers will not only want you but pay you more as well. If you're just doing as asked you'll be 'racing to the bottom'.

Practice interviews. Teach your client how to keep focused on what they want – both the outcome and the process. Get them to a point where they enjoy talking about their positive achievements in a confident and credible manner. First, conduct at least one practice interview with them and give them as much opportunity as possible to rehearse their prepared answers with you. Encourage them to practice with friends and family as well. Between you, think of different questions which would draw on the same information, e.g. the same 'case study' may illustrate both the ability to develop effective working relationships and the ability to deal with difficult people. This will ensure they are well-prepared and give them confidence. The more they have ready prepared, the more 'brain space' they will have left for dealing with the unexpected.

Preparation for tests. Some organizations use tests as part of their selection process. These might be personality tests or capability tests such as verbal or numerical reasoning. They are particularly common in graduate recruitment.

Some 'golden rules' for completing tests:

• Read and ensure they understand the scoring system and each question before answering.
• Read and ensure they understand the scoring system and each question before answering!
• Yes, read and ensure they understand the scoring system and each question before answering! There is no surer way to do badly than to think a score of '1' means 'totally disagree' when it means 'agree completely'!
• Ensure they know what the time scale is so that they give themselves a chance to answer all questions. If it's a capability test work carefully but quickly. If they get stuck on a question go on to the next and come back later.
• If it is a personality test go with their intuitive answer, don't spend ages analyzing and poring over each question
• In a personality test don't try to give the answers that they think the organization expects – be true to themselves. For a start these tests contain checks for consistency, and what is the point in ending up in a job that they are unsuited for and unlikely to be happy doing?
• Practice, especially for ability tests – for instance examples can be found at: http://www.shldirect.com/practice_tests.html

Assessment centers

Some organizations, especially for more senior posts or even graduate schemes use comprehensive assessment centers covering for instance, an interview, capability and/or personality tests, a meeting of the candidates to discuss and resolve a business problem, an analysis exercise where data about a business problem is presented and recommendations have to be developed for a way forward. Presentations based either on this or on a subject of the candidate's choice are fairly common. Again help your coachee prepare thoroughly.

Psychological preparation

Here are two options which you can use, either or both may be helpful: visualization and Cognitive Behavioral Coaching (CBC).

Visualization. This technique works particularly well for preparing for interviews, or indeed any meeting, such as a networking meeting. They should visualize themselves being successful at the interview – walk them through the process from start to finish, imagining themselves going confidently into the building where they will be interviewed, being greeted, answering questions confidently and clearly and then their feelings as they come out of the interview. Get them to really focus on the feeling they want to have as they walk out – it might be 'proud and confident, knowing I've done my best and made all the points I want to make'. Again, get them to do this from the identity of the role they have applied for.

Encourage them to get themselves to the point where they really enjoy talking about their achievements and feel so confident with their answers a little frisson of excitement (decide their own positive emotion) goes through them when they think about the interview.

Cognitive Behavioral Coaching (CBC). CBC has its roots in Cognitive Behavioral Therapy (CBT), which is credited to psychiatrist Aaron Temkin Beck (Curwen, Palmer and Ruddell, 2000). Back in the 1960s, Beck noticed that patients talked to themselves in an 'internal dialogue', of which they were not always fully aware. However, they could learn to identify, report and consequently change their thoughts into more helpful ones. A little voice on the shoulder saying 'Who do you think you are to be going for a job like that?' can be changed to something like 'With all the things you've achieved over the last five years you are highly qualified for that job'. The premise is that it is not the situation itself that is the problem but the individual's thoughts and feelings and the meaning they give it which then influences their behavior (McMahon and Archer, 2010). The CBC model has been developed in the UK by McMahon, Palmer, Dryden and Neenan.

It is so powerful because it develops their awareness of the way they think, its benefits and limitations, and helps them develop alternatives which serve them better. They learn to identify the 'cognitive distortions' they are applying (Dryden and Neenan, 2004), for instance:

- Discounting the positive – 'I know I did that practice well but I'll be hopeless on the day'
- Fortune telling – 'I know it'll be terrible'
- Should, Must, Have to and Ought (victim language) – 'I must apply for it because there aren't many jobs about'
- Generalizations – 'I'm always hopeless at interviews'.

Here is a case study to illustrate how CBC or 'guided discovery' (McMahon, 2006) works.

Case study: Claudine

Claudine was really worried and nervous about having to give a presentation as part of the selection process for a job she really wanted. She kept thinking about a couple of her colleagues who she saw as fantastic presenters – really funny, engaging and knowledgeable – and comparing herself unfavorably. These thoughts then made her feel useless and stupid so she became nervous and self-conscious. That meant in her presentations she was unconsciously holding back on what she could really do – which was also very engaging, but in a different way to their style. Through questioning I helped her become aware of these thoughts and feelings and the impact on her presentation skills (behavior) and then to change them to more productive ones (see Figure 5.3).

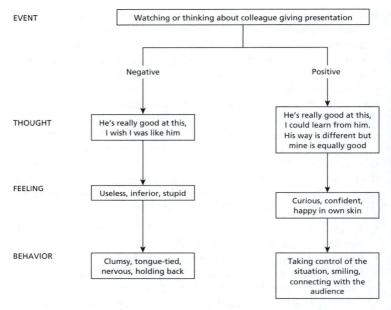

EVENT

Watching or thinking about colleague giving presentation

Negative

Positive

THOUGHT

He's really good at this, I wish I was like him

He's really good at this, I could learn from him. His way is different but mine is equally good

FEELING

Useless, inferior, stupid

Curious, confident, happy in own skin

BEHAVIOR

Clumsy, tongue-tied, nervous, holding back

Taking control of the situation, smiling, connecting with the audience

Figure 5.3 Cognitive Behavioural Coaching (CBC) – example

This same technique can be used to address any other factors that may be hampering your client, e.g. lack of confidence, perfectionism, lack of self-esteem, interview nerves, thoughts about being made redundant.

Step by step guide to using CBC in this context (adapted from Debra Jinks, 2011)

1 Explore the current situation:

   – Tell me about the situation that is concerning you
   – What thoughts are going through your head as you think about that? What are you believing is true about yourself and the situation?
   – How are you feeling as those thoughts run through your mind?
   – What do you do, or not do, as a result of those thoughts and feelings?

– How are all these things connected?
– What thoughts, beliefs and behaviors might be inhibiting you?

2 Challenge and change:

– What would be a different way of thinking about this? What could you believe instead?
– What would be the consequences if you did that?
– What evidence is there for your new belief(s)? What would support your new way of thinking?
– What else can you do to generate evidence to support your new way of thinking and beliefs?

3 Explore consequences:

– How might you perform now, with these new thoughts, beliefs, feelings and behaviors?
– What can you do to help you maintain your new way of thinking, feeling and behaving?

Help your coachee to put together a personal development plan which will embed their new ways of thinking and behaving.

On the day of the interview

Once again, coach them through both the practicalities and the psychological aspects of this, for instance, have they planned how they will get there in good time? How will they deal with their nerves?

Decision making about options and offers

It is that great moment when your client has an offer – or even offers – to consider. Your role is to:

• Explore and help them to be conscious of their normal decision-making methods and offer them more helpful ones if appropriate. Surprisingly, many people do not consciously know how they make decisions or have a limited repertoire which could be expanded to help them make better choices.

- It is *not* your job to tell them or even hint or suggest what they should do. It's important the client feels comfortable with the decision they have taken so they need a method that suits them and *it must be their decision.*

NLP talks of 'convincer patterns' (Knight, 2009) – what does it take for someone to choose a course of action? These are influenced by the way we each take in information and so we all have different preferences. The main ones are visual demonstration or presentation, auditory explanation or discussion, active experimentation, detailed exploration or simply allowing time for the whole thing to sink in. Or it may be a combination of these. By reviewing past successful decisions with them they can learn what works for them.

You can help by offering some decision-making methods or you may know your client well enough by now to know what is likely to work best for them:

1 Ask great questions:

   - How will you feel in 12 months' time if you say yes (or no) to this?
   - How do you think your life will be in one, two, five or ten years' time if you say yes (or no) to this?
   - What is the worst (or best) that can happen if you say yes (or no) to this?
   - What would have to happen for you to say yes (or no) to this?
   - What is stopping you?
   - Suppose time and money were limitless, what would you do?
   - If you did know what to do, what would you do?
   - If you chose to do X, what might be the benefits (or drawbacks)?
   - If you do nothing, what do you think might happen?

2 Offer some logical, structured options such as listing pros and cons, rating or ranking factors for and against.

3 Share stories about how you have made decisions or how others with similar dilemmas have decided and what the consequences were – many people find it enlightening to know how others with similar ambitions have made their decisions and got to where they want to go.

4 Go back to their criteria about what is important for them, for instance, their career satisfaction drivers – ensure it meets enough of these and is going to lead to their ultimate career goal if it is just a stepping stone.

5 Use a gestalt approach, which enables the best decision to emerge, rather than being forced (Leary-Joyce, 2010).

A gestalt method of decision making

– Take a piece of A4 paper – placing it in landscape, draw a line down the middle.

– Ask the client to put the heading 'take the job' (or whatever the first option is) on one side and on the other write the alternative, or one of the alternatives. It may be 'don't take the job' or 'continue in current job', or something quite different.

– Get them to explore one side of the dilemma first – draw or write on that side of the paper all the things that come up for them when they think about taking that option. You can ask developing questions such as 'what are you seeing, hearing, feeling?' if necessary. They can even use colored pens.

– Now move to the other side, the other option, and do the same.

– Ask what they are noticing – let their attention go from one to the other and add anything else that comes up.

– As they do this the answer will emerge – they are relying on their intuition to find out what is right for them.

Negotiating terms

A decision to accept an offer then brings another dilemma – the negotiation about the employment package. It's not the place of this book to teach in-depth negotiation skills so I will just cover some principles which, in my experience, have proved important in the career transition context:

• People who estimate their worth more highly and ask for higher salaries get paid more; this is partly to do with what Daniel Kahneman (2011) calls 'anchoring' – whatever figure they mention will be the number the

person holds in their mind, both consciously and unconsciously. It may come down from that but you can be sure
it won't go up from a low figure! Also remember they will
never again have such a good opportunity with that
company to negotiate the best possible salary and
package. Once inside, there are generally far more restric-
tions on pay budgets, salary ranges, etc.

* They may need to deal with unhelpful beliefs they
hold about negotiation, e.g. that they are no good at it,
that it's necessary to make instant decisions when
made an offer. Again you could use CBC to help them deal
with these.

* Ensure they don't feel pressured to give an instant
response to an offer and are comfortable asking for time
to consider.

* A useful technique for deciding what is an acceptable
salary, based on Kahneman's anchoring, is to give them a
number and ask whether the salary should be higher or
lower. Give out a range of numbers and again a feel for
what is acceptable will emerge.

Self-employment

Life is like an experiment – try it, get involved, see
which bits you like and which you don't. I do that a lot.
I went with the flow of what came rather than defining
a niche – the world was too big for me to do that. I left
full-time employment five years ago and now I've got a
clearer idea of how it all fits – I'm pulling the reins
together, like work streams, threads.

Angela Watson, Careers After Forty Coach at
PGD Coaching Solutions

I experienced coaching in 2006 and knew in the back of
my mind that was what I wanted to do so I trained and
came out thinking 'Hey, I'm a life coach!' Pretty soon I
realized I needed a niche and initially I chose career
coaching because I really understood this with my HR
background in corporate environments and my own
career change story. I now work more and more with

people transitioning into running their own business because that's the experience I can now share.

Karen Williams, Self Discovery Coaching

Two very different approaches to setting up in business, yet similarly compelling personal stories.

So where would you start in helping someone set out on the road to self-employment, be it freelancing, contracting or working as an associate? There is much 'conventional wisdom' and many a 'fool-proof formula' around about the best ways of doing this. Yet as Angela and Karen demonstrate, different approaches do work for different people.

So here I will talk about the essentials you'll need to cover with anyone setting up in self-employment and give you some options for how you approach this. You can then choose a way which works for you and your clients. It will most likely be a combination of your own preferences and training and theirs. Many of the principles and challenges are the same as for finding a new role so you can also refer back to the earlier part of the chapter.

This book is not intended to be a comprehensive guide to self-employment so you will need to develop your own knowledge and information sources so that you can guide the focus and thinking of your coachee. Some useful information sources are provided.

Overall approach

Your overall approach may be anywhere along a spectrum from highly logical and structured to exploratory and 'emergent'. And indeed it may vary between these at particular stages in the process and for different purposes.

A logical process will work through in a structured way:

- The individual – what they want to gain from self-employment and will they be suited to it?
- The business idea – market opportunities, business model
- Practicalities – business plan, company formation, financial and other resources
- Winning business – bringing together all of the above.

An emergent, exploratory approach, which is what Angela Watson uses with her clients, will go where the client's energy is, sharing stories with them, helping them find stories of how it's worked for others and ultimately helping them create their own.

In this section I will look at both approaches and techniques you can use, but 'structurally' I will follow the logical approach, as I believe that is what most of you will find easier to follow here. I start with an assumption that your client has already developed their vision and Well Formed Outcome (WFO) or goal and is now starting to explore the practicalities of achieving self-employment.

The other thing to bear in mind is that setting up in self-employment may be a long journey – it took me over ten years to take the plunge and it's been the same for many others although the reasons may be different.

Andy Britnell, blogging and social media coach, developed a very clear picture of the skills and experience he would need to run his own business and identified a strategy to achieve them. He used his corporate life to develop what he needed – when he arrived in sales he told his boss that he was not there to make a career, he just wanted to 'get the tee shirt' and develop skills he would need for the future.

An emergent, transitional approach based on taking action to test out possible futures is very much part of Herminia Ibarra's thesis in *Working Identity: Unconventional Strategies for Reinventing Your Career* (2003). When Angela Watson discovered this book this struck a chord with her own experience.

It's all about you

This is the key thing about self-employment – it really is all about you! Which can be both exciting and daunting, and is not appropriate for everyone. Three things from my own research and experience of self-employment stick in my mind –

- 'Think about it – then think some more' (Johnson, 2005)
- 'You need lots of self . . . self-starting, self-inspired, self-directed' (Oglethorpe, 2012)

- It most likely won't work out at all in the way you expect so you really have to be open to outcomes and possibilities while having an overarching vision.

So the first step for the client is to think seriously about their suitability. Develop their awareness of:

- What it is about them that will make them successful in self-employment
- What may make them less successful.
- Whether those 'risks' can be managed, whether they are prepared to manage them – and how.

Show them how to collect some data, test it out, talk about it and think about it. Four possible options for this are:

1 SWOT – just as good a starting point for thinking about self-employment as it is for employment. Using it to determine an individual's aptitude and motivation for self-employment can be very helpful.
2 Self-assessment questionnaire, with honest input from those who know them well, and from your knowledge of them.
3 Personality profiles – which provide tried and tested profiles which are normed against large populations.
4 An experimental, experiential, emergent approach. Using Emergent knowledge techniques, such as Clean Networks, if you are trained in these, or work with these same principles if you are not.

Taking each of these in turn:

1 SWOT – exactly the same process, benefits, pros and cons apply as for finding a new role. Ensure they really do get clear on what their passions are and their unique talents as these will be the key to being successful as they branch out alone and make people want to do business with them. Time and again this has been found to be the number one factor in a successful business.
2 Self-assessment questionnaire – you can develop your own questionnaire based on your own knowledge and experience and/or books and websites about

self-employment. Here are some headings to give you a starting point: Personal skills, attitudes, values and aptitudes, Personal circumstances, What are you prepared to give and to give up.

Useful lists are given in the following books: *Is Self-Employment for You?* (Casey, 2004) and *The Independent Consultant's Survival Guide: Starting up and Succeeding as a Self-employed Consultant* (Johnson, 2005). There are plenty of others available – you may already have your own favorite.

3 Personality profiles – tried and tested, validated and normed against large populations. Again, you may have personal preferences. Two options which Andy Britnell uses are 'Insights' and 'Motivational Maps'.

'Insights' is based on the work of Jung, using four colors to represent behavioral preferences: cool blue, fiery red, sunshine yellow and earth green. Motivational Maps evolved from Maslow and Schein's work. They identify the individual's top three motivators and their least preferred. Andy's own strong preferences for Creator (desire for freedom and creativity), Expert (loves to learn) and Searcher (search for meaning rather than money), combined with a low preference for Defender (stability, security and safety), fit him well for running his combination of constantly evolving small businesses as part of a portfolio life.

There is no 'ideal' profile for self-employment – the point is to think about what the profile means and how it will fit with the life and business the client desires.

4 Emergent techniques such as the gestalt method detailed above or Emergent Knowledge techniques such as Clean Networks which is given below in the section on choosing a business model.

As a result some will decide *not* to go ahead, for instance because they realize they like the security of a regular income and that being self-employed is therefore not for them. You may need to help them come to terms with this.

The business idea

It is time to explore big picture business topics such as market opportunities and business model.

Subjects to get your client thinking about on their business proposition:

- What problems are you helping people to solve – why would they buy at all?
- Who is the ideal customer for these products or services – how will you narrow your focus to those who really might buy from you? You can't be all things to all people, especially if you intend to work on your own.
- How do your talents and skills help you solve these problems in a unique way – why would they buy from *you*? What you are offering, as such, is probably not unique, so why choose to buy it from you?

In my experience many people who want to become self-employed know what they want to do, and what they want their life to be like, but haven't framed it in terms that will be useful to potential customers.

Some techniques to use here:

- *Visualization* – what is your ideal customer like? What *specifically* are the problems that keep them awake at night that you can help them solve? Who are they?
- *Walk in their shoes* – actually move to a different place in the room, a different seat. Imagine you are now them, talk from their point of view – let's call the customer Ron to avoid confusion. What am I, Ron, stressing about? What help do I want? What would make me take action? What sort of person or business do I like to work with? What would really put me off working with someone?
- *Take an objective view* – move your client to yet another place in the room and ask them to look at themselves and Ron from that vantage point. What would they say to 'themselves' as a third party? Have they got a clear idea about what they are offering? How valuable is it to potential customers? To Ron – would you buy from X? Why would you? What else needs to happen for you to buy from X? (They may be able to answer the questions from

that vantage point or may need to move back to their own or Ron's seat.) What advice would you give to X?

- You may need to get them to alternate between these viewpoints several times as they adjust things to a point where they are happy. It is quite likely that they will need to revisit their proposition several times later as it evolves.

The business model

Your client needs to decide on the business model, or combination of models, they will use. The main choices of business model are discussed fully in Chapter 8 where business models for career transition coaching are considered.

The purpose here is to give you some techniques to help your client decide what will work for them. Here are some options to choose from, which you can select based on your client's preferences:

1 Develop a list of pros and cons and weigh these up, either intuitively or by rating
2 Use the gestalt-based method discussed earlier in this chapter
3 Use another emergent, exploratory technique:–

   – Take each option in turn and get them to write it on a post-it note. Let's start with 'Freelancing'.
   – Ask them to place the post-it wherever seems right to them. Get them to check that it is in the best position by asking in turn 'Is it at the right ... height, angle, direction, and so on. For instance they may stick it on the back of the door and then adjust it from somewhere in the middle to near the bottom.
   – Then tell them to place themselves in a space that feels right for them – this might end up as somewhere far across the other side of the room where they can hardly see it.
   – Ask, 'And what do you know about Freelancing from that space there?' Ask a supplementary question if it seems helpful: 'What else do you know from that space there?' Anything can emerge! They may find it seems very remote, that they are unconnected with it ... or

perhaps that, although it seems small and far away, they are very curious about it and want to find out more.

- Once they have explored from that place ask them to move to another space that feels right for them. Ask the same question(s). Exploring it from a different position will give them a different perspective.
- Move them to six different positions, asking the same questions, and finally get them to go back to where they started, again asking what they know now.
- Finish by asking 'And what difference does that knowing make?'
- Do the same for each option.

This is based on 'Clean Networks', an 'Emergent Knowledge' (EK) technique, developed by David Grove (Grove and Wilson, 2005). It uses 'the power of six' which has also been written about by Philip Harland (2009). Angela Watson uses it very successfully with her clients at PGD Coaching Solutions. She finds that by physically moving and gently exploring the issue the client also finds they are moving in pursuit of their goal. The microcosm (of the exercise) reflects the macrocosm (of their goal)! This reflects two of the principles of 'Emergent Knowledge' – that the client's psyche is part of a system and when one part changes it impacts the others. David Grove believed that this 'psychescape' as he called it, was physical as well as mental. It also reflects the principle of 'six degrees of separation', that everyone in the world is separated by only six connections.

You can use it for many other purposes as well, e.g. to explore and develop the initial goal, to change a barrier or blockage, prepare for an interview.

To use this and other Emergent Knowledge techniques most effectively you do need to train. In its full form there is a particular syntax, pace, tone and wording but you can still achieve some good results by following the process above. My own training in Emergent Knowledge has enriched my coaching significantly, as has Clean Language. However, I recognize that, just like any other tool or technique, it's not for everyone. If you do want to pursue it further an excellent option is Angela Dunbar's teleclasses, including free tasters (http://www.cleancoaching.com/).

Practicalities

Time to look at practicalities such as the business plan, company formation (limited company, sole trader, partnership?), financial and other resources. There are many sources of information and training about different aspects of company formation available which you need to be knowledgeable about such as:

- Government organizations and websites, e.g. Business Link and HMRC (Her Majesty's Revenue and Customs) in the UK
- Membership organizations such as Chambers of Commerce
- Private businesses and websites, e.g. accountancy firms, company formation agencies, banks.

You can point them to specific sources of information and in the direction of their network to get recommendations for services such as accountancy and legal advice. Set them to work to research what is best for them and their business.

Winning business: Brand, marketing and selling

Exactly the same lessons apply as when setting out to get a new employed role and the same issues will arise. Develop brand and identity, get networking, talk to people, learn! Shift identity, deal with limiting beliefs. You can use all the same approaches discussed in the section above on employment.

Retirement

Once again support with both practical and psychological matters is important. Clients need to think about the obvious question of their finances but equally about the psychological transition – often the loss of social interaction is the most difficult aspect in Gerry O'Neill's experience, together with loss of status and identity, especially if leaving a senior position. Retirement is increasingly meaning different things, especially with changes in pension rules, reduction in pension benefits and the removal of default retirement ages.

It may be that your client is not thinking about retiring yet but in five, ten or 15 years' time. They may want help in planning how to get there. I have used a timeline very successfully here – getting the client to write down points along it and where they need to be. For instance, I had one client who was running his own business and wanted to retire in 15 years' time. I got him to think about where his business and personal life needed to be in five years and then in ten years for him to achieve this. For instance he knew he had to find and develop his successor as Executive Chairman.

Key points from this chapter

- This is not a content-free zone – you need to know 'the rules of the game': to be knowledgeable about employment and self-employment practices such as CV preparation, interview techniques, social networking and sources of information such as company structures.
- Whilst providing information, knowledge, guidance and options for your client, beware of telling them what to do and taking responsibility for their decisions.
- Keys to success at this stage are self-assessment, opportunity assessment, self-branding, marketing, selling, negotiation and decision making.
- Both structured, logical and more exploratory, emergent approaches can work, according to the preferences of your client and your own style of working.
- You can help on both a practical and psychological level.
- Helping your client find a good state is critical to success in undertaking all aspects of this stage and many clients will find some elements very challenging, for instance selling themselves at interview or in a CV.
- The mind-set needed is to sell themselves and their achievements and put themselves into the shoes of others.
- It may be a long journey, and take many years for the client to achieve their ultimate goal, especially if it is to move to self-employment. Reasons for this can be many and varied, from needing to build financial security, to needing to try out different identities, to resolving limiting beliefs.

Challenging transitions

The course of a career doesn't run smoothly. This chapter looks at the more challenging aspects of career transition – situations you might encounter and some approaches used by successful career transition coaches. I should also say that this is not setting out to be 'a balanced view', weighing up the pros and cons – it is looking at the downsides, the challenges, and how you can counter them.

I have divided the chapter up into:

1 The transition itself

  – Redundancy or redeployment

2 Personal characteristics of the client which make career transition a challenge

  – Senior executives
  – Young, inexperienced people, from graduates to NEETs (Not in Education, Employment or Training)
  – Older people
  – Being part of a 'minority group' – ethnic, religious, sex or disability

3 Psychological or behavioral challenges – These may be long-standing or develop as a result of their career transition experience.

  – Dealing with failure
  – Resistant, won't engage or feel stuck
  – Don't take action
  – Low confidence/self-esteem

- Expect too much from you as their coach – either action or support
- Identity issues.

The transition itself

Redundancy and redeployment

Gerry O'Neill of Penna, one of the UK's leading outplacement services providers, sums up your job here as to help your client make their change curve as short and shallow as possible: to move quickly to secure their next career move and get on with their lives.

How the client initially presents to the coach can vary enormously: at worst some may start in floods of tears, others want to vent their anger – a good career coach needs to have very strong EQ or Emotional Quotient (Goleman, 1998). Needs and expectations vary enormously too – some want to do blue sky thinking, others will say 'just tell me what to do'. Some expect you do the work for them! Hence the importance of establishing the psychological contract at the outset, says Gerry. 'This is how we'll work together, it's a partnership – this is what I offer, what will you bring to achieve your outcomes?' The key is to get the client to think about and understand him or herself and build their confidence – who am I? What can I offer? What's important to me? Challenge and sometimes 'tough love' is part of the relationship, helping clients find out more about what they think they want to do, enabling them to test out their perceptions, ensuring they do the work that is necessary.

Workshops and coaching give them opportunities for this, for instance, specialist workshops on subjects such as self-employment. These give valuable information and a real sense of what it's like to work for oneself. Sometimes after attending a client will recognize that it's not for them – a positive outcome! Better to find out sooner rather than later. Sometimes the coach has to push the client back along the change curve – if you sense they are jumping into a new role too quickly just because their leaving date is imminent, without researching and testing, they may be unhappy with that in six months' time. Time to say 'Let's check this out'.

Deni Lyall of Winning Performance builds in what she calls a reality check for people who want to consider doing something new; it comes down to a reconciliation of four things:

1 What skills do they have?
2 What do they want in ten years' time? What are their aspirations?
3 What are their current family and financial commitments, such as mortgage, children's education?
4 What is available in the market at the moment?

She often sends them off to research their chosen options, for instance someone who wants to be a freelancer has to go and talk to five people who are freelancers and five companies who use them – find out what it's really like to do it and what organizations are actually looking for. She also shares her own experiences and contacts.

She finds that about 50 percent of her clients these days opt for employment whereas ten years ago it was 95 percent.

A few people want to take some time out before deciding what they want to do but they have special circumstances which enable them to do this, such as being over 50, having a lot of money behind them or a partner with a very well-paid job – most people have a mortgage to pay so don't have this luxury. Deni sometimes feels the attitudes of family and friends can be unhelpful – being told 'You can do whatever you want now' is not always practical, and only about 25 percent really see it as an opportunity for a significant change. Some people feel embarrassed that they just want the same job again and need reassurance that this is OK.

Once they have really tested out and decided what they want to do, the next challenge is to ensure their work experience and achievements look and feel good to them. Deni does this by looking for the real value of what they have done, getting to the business benefit of it and positioning it in a way an employer will understand. A lot of the coaching role is about reframing and finding a positioning that is truly congruent for them. When you find this you both know it – they are off and running. Employers are looking for very round pegs for round holes given the number of people job-hunting, so it is relatively easy for those with solid experience and achievements to sell themselves. However, those who have moved around or have been stuck in a role where they've been able to make little contribution for a couple of years need more help.

Deni's experienced eye enables her to counter what might tell against her client. Getting this across in a CV and ensuring that it's is not just a job description is where Deni finds she sometimes really needs to focus. She describes her approach as 'tough love', when her client needs to dig deep to articulate what they have that will get them the job they want. She finds clients appreciate her robustness because she knows that 'with a rubbish CV they will get nowhere'.

This seems something of a contradiction of what Deni says is often her major role, which is to help them feel a worthy person again. But being pushed to think about what they personally contributed and the value their business got from it really does make them feel good about themselves. Having a great CV also enables them to polish up the conversations they will have when networking and with potential employers about the value they have added and what they do and do not want next. It's a real shaping exercise, an absolutely bedrock thing according to Deni.

She finds most people take six months to find a job when made redundant and she knows that some of the people she sees will take a lot longer. The good news is that those who are energetic, proactive and voice their views *will* get one. For people who are quiet, reticent and do not tend to voice their opinion, the current job market is less charitable. Some coaching or interview practice would be invaluable to them. People are much more accustomed to changing jobs these days, except perhaps those who have had long-standing jobs in the public sector.

Deni finds the biggest challenge for most people is networking. Often they don't understand what it means so don't make use of its full potential and dislike doing it because they think it is just about asking for a job. Often Deni has to spend time with them going through actual networking situations until they have a breakthrough in their understanding and tune into what it is really about. For instance with one client she firmly suggested that they find three people higher up than them and ask their views on where those people would see them, how they regarded them and what they saw them doing. It was working on the actual questions they could ask those contacts that really helped. Clients need to understand that networking is a *focused conversation* and that, in Deni's experience, 80 percent of people get jobs through networking and for the self-employed 75 percent of work comes from people they know. It's not about marketing, selling and expensive websites; it's about getting advice and information.

Personal characteristics

Senior executives

You might be surprised to see senior executives mentioned here. What do they have to worry about? Paese and Wellins (2007) found that senior executives rated transitions at work as their top life challenge – 19 percent, compared with just less than 15 percent citing bereavement! Stefan Cantore, Senior Fellow Leadership and Organizational Development at the Office for Public Management, speaking at the University of East London in 2011, identified four types of career transitions that senior executives face (after Dotlich, Noel and Walker 2004): role change, or loss, and personal change, or loss.

What are the challenges here?

About them

- They are accustomed to being successful and having people around them doing their routine work. Psychologically it may feel humiliating and in practical matters they may be fairly helpless, in particular lacking in IT skills.

- Personality traits, both positive and their 'dark side', may work against them – what helped them succeed also leads to their downfall. According to Adrian Furnham (2011) as many leaders fail as succeed and many of the highly successful have a dark side often associated with 'narcissism and moral imbecility'. He identifies competencies and their dark sides, such as 'action oriented', which can have a reckless, dictatorial aspect, as well as six personality disorders which may be present in senior leaders – antisocial/psychopathic, narcissistic, paranoid, schizoid, histrionic and obsessive compulsive disorders. Others such as Goldman (2006) and Khoo and Burch (2008) have also researched personality disorders in leaders.
- Furnham also found patterns which derail high potentials involving their demonstrated strengths, organizational complicity and the resultant derailing flaws. For instance a senior manager with a good track record and action focus will find their flaws ignored while they produce the results. Ultimately though they are likely to be overwhelmed by complexity and their lack of strategic focus will lead to a decline in performance which will not be forgiven.
- Senior managers may lack insight into themselves and how they are truly perceived – although they will have experienced years of feedback through performance reviews, 360 degree feedback and employee surveys, they got to their successful position by being as they are and that is the strongest feedback they could have about what works.
- In addition to being senior they are also likely to be older so have those challenges as well.
- Many will have built their success on 'traditional' approaches to management and leadership and have a personal style that enjoys certainty and discipline – these won't serve them well either in being out of work or in the likely requirements of a new role.

About the market

- Global markets and businesses are changing and new styles of leadership and management are expected (see Chapter 1). Not only do they need to change but they need to be capable of leading the change in others.

- Increasingly, leading change is the main role of a leader and its focus is human, not process as in the past.
- Employers are often reluctant to recruit older senior executives – according to Mays and Sloane (2011) the reasons for this are mainly: inflexible management style, difficulty reporting to a younger boss, high compensation needs and a lack of IT skills.

The focus in coaching them

- Help them make sense of trends in the global market and their sector and to consider the implications for them in the short, medium and long term.
- Draw on their experience and learning from previous transitions they have negotiated. Recognize the value of these as sources of wisdom and confidence.
- Help them 'learn how to learn' (Cantore, 2011) through skills of self-reflection which will serve them well in the longer term. Get them to put these skills to use in understanding their overused strengths, dark sides and other potential derailers, plus developing the leadership thinking and behaviors required for twenty-first century leadership.
- Guide them on developing practical skills and/or where to find them, for instance through a Virtual Assistant.
- Networking – develop their understanding of how it can benefit them in the broadest sense, from support and encouragement to actually finding a new role. Help develop their skills and confidence to engage in it. Offer support from your own network.
- Encourage them to consider wider options – taking a step back and thinking about what they want at this stage in their career, thinking about alternatives – perhaps as a short-term option to get back into the market and to establish contacts. For instance, they could act as a consultant or interim, or work in a smaller company as they are less likely than corporates to hire from within (Mays and Sloane, 2011).

- Work with them to develop their story. Gabriel, Gray and Goregaokar (2010), researching the experiences of unemployed executives, found that those who coped best had an open-ended narrative where they saw their situation as a temporary aberration or regarded career and life as different things, in contrast to those who saw their job loss as the 'end of the line'. Ibarra (2003; Ibarra and Lineback, 2005) developed this concept of 'story telling' in a highly positive way.
- Help them anticipate and then counter objections against employing them because of their age. In fact, make their age an asset – focus on characteristics such as problem solving and judgment (Mays and Sloane, 2011).
- Contract well and stick with it unless you both agree to re-contract. Ensure their understanding of what you are offering, what it will take from them and the outcomes they can expect from the coaching. Be mindful of the role and status they have had and the expectations this will have set up in them.

Young, inexperienced people: From graduates to NEETs (Not in Education, Employment or Training)

What are the challenges here?

About them

- Lack of the experience and skills employers are looking for, plus lack of qualifications in the case of NEETs. Figures for the third quarter of 2011 showed almost one in five 16 to 24 year olds in England were NEETs (Department for Education, 2011).
- Attitude and expectations of Generation Y, the Millennials, and the upcoming Generation Z. It's common wisdom that they have been brought up with a sense of entitlement, believe they are the best and that it's impossible to fail. They don't want to start at the bottom or work unsocial or long hours – in fact they see their work as an extension of their social life and expect a 'celebrity'

career – the X Factor generation. They want flexibility, and quick results in terms of skills and salary progression, expecting to change jobs every two to three years. According to Rosemary Haefner (Levinson, 2008) Human Resources VP at CareerBuilder, Gen Y can't tolerate uncertainty and ambiguity, they expect immediate answers.

- They have never experienced the type of challenges presented by a weak economy. The climate they have been brought up in which resulted in those attitudes and expectations will make this particularly testing for them, with their limited experience, lack of coping skills and dislike of uncertainty (Levinson, 2008).
- There is also a pessimism about younger people and their prospects. In *Jilted Generation* (2010) Ed Howker and Shiv Malik look at their peers and see what they call 'a quiet depression that is happening daily'. They claim middle-class people who should be doing well don't know what to do with their lives. Even Katja Hall, chief policy director of the Confederation of British Industry, is quoted by the BBC (Harrison, 2011) referring to the vast scale of the problem to be overcome to avoid a lost generation.
- Even in the best of times few young people are given the opportunity to develop the skills to succeed in interviews, present themselves, etc. as part of their education.

About the market

- 'It's the economy, stupid' (after James Carville and Bill Clinton) . . .
- Leaving college during a downturn has a large, negative and long-lasting impact – that is for the first 20 years of a career, resulting in lower-level occupations, lower earnings and slightly longer tenure for higher educational attainment (Kahn, 2009).
- High and growing levels of unemployment, especially youth unemployment – both a real impact and leading to feelings of hopelessness about getting a job.
- Shifts in the labor market (Sissons, 2011).

- Employers wanting something for nothing – the growth of serial, unpaid internships which don't necessarily lead to a permanent, paid role.
- Reduced education and employment budgets resulting, in the UK, in cuts to careers services, and reduced 1:1 tuition for pupils falling behind in reading, writing and math. Also a 75 percent reduction in financial support for the 'entitlement funding grant' which helps sixth formers with university and college choices and the end of the Connexions employment service (Shepherd, 2011).

The focus in coaching them

- Developing and bringing out their 'employability' (CBI, 2007).
- Helping them to understand employer expectations, the job market and how to sell themselves. There is no excuse for a lack of knowledge about the organization they are applying to with all that's available on the internet – not only information but opportunities for interaction and engagement, for instance through 'Liking' them on Facebook.
- Ensure they get the basics right – often they make simple mistakes such as delivering a poorly presented CV containing spelling mistakes or turning up to interviews in casual dress.
- Developing optimism and confidence and helping them not to just settle for something below their capabilities. Lisa Kahn (2009) asserts that to pursue a career which meets their potential in a weak economy they need the right mind-set.

The fundamental difference is that they have less to work with so it's even more essential to

- Bring out what they do have
- Understand the easy things they can do which make a huge difference (spell-checking their CV for instance)
- Help them find opportunities to build up what they are missing and

- Develop realistic expectations for the short term at least, which may mean taking a 'detour' to get to what they really want if it gives them confidence, experience and skills they need for their ideal role.

Like other age groups, as Deni Lyall says, 'they have only got what they've got and they can only have what's available'. But that doesn't mean you can't help them develop both a tactical solution and a longer-term strategy. All the approaches and tools covered previously in this book can be used, plus you need to be knowledgeable about opportunities specifically open to young people, for instance the Prince's Trust and Striding Out for personal and business development, the UK government's Get Britain Working initiative (http://www.dwp.gov.uk/policy/welfare-reform/get-britain-working/), Prospects website for graduate jobs and courses (http://www.prospects.ac.uk/), graduate job sites such as in national newspapers and following companies they are interested in through their websites, Facebook and so on.

Older people: Employment, self-employment, portfolio, retirement?

I guess the first question to ask is how old actually are 'older people'? Traditionally it has been thought that getting a new job over 40 is difficult. Yet the trend now is for people in their sixties or beyond who would previously have retired still wanting to work. Sometimes it is because they feel they are forced to work due to reduced pension benefits and fears about not having enough money in retirement (Munnell, Webb, and Golub-Sass, 2007). For others it is a choice to continue putting their energy into paid work.

Clearly there is a difference in mind-set between those voluntarily seeking a career or job change and those who find themselves unemployed, particularly those who are unemployed and have limited education. In the US, 2009 figures show that 10.8 percent of people aged 65 or over who had not completed high school were unemployed, compared with only 5.8 percent of those with four or more years of college education (Johnson and Mommaerts, 2009). That said, unemployment rates are generally lower for older workers than young ones, although the rates are rising partly as a reflection of there being more older people remaining in the workforce.

Older men tend to spend longer out of work when made redundant than their younger counterparts, although there is not a significant difference for women. According to the US Bureau of Labor Statistics (cited in Johnson, 2009) 44 percent of unemployed men aged 55 to 64 had been unemployed for at least 27 weeks. By comparison, only 36 percent of unemployed men aged 35 to 44 had spent 27 or more weeks seeking work. The reasons for this are not well understood but Johnson (2009) surmises that it may be due to a combination of factors – less intensive and effective job search, being more selective about what they want, reluctance of employers to hire them, or even discrimination by employers against them. Johnson also notes that when older workers eventually find a new job, they usually earn much less than they did previously – what better case for career transition coaching!

Here are the challenges for older people:

About them

- Lack of experience in looking for a new role. This may apply across the spectrum of jobs – if they have been successful, especially in a senior position, jobs will have come looking for them or if they have been in a 'job for life' in the public sector they will not have needed to change
- Inability to identify and summarize their assets and transferable skills
- Lack of understanding of how the job market works, especially the importance, purpose and skill of successful networking
- Pessimism about their ability to find a new role at their age if seeking to be employed
- Lack of flexibility about trying something new, or lack of skills such as IT and social media
- Feelings of failure and humiliation if made redundant, especially for the first time

- Feel they have a lot to lose, for instance in pensions benefits, if they have been with a single employer for a long time and want to change direction
- If they have not been in the job market for some time they will find it has changed enormously – when they last searched jobs were probably advertised in newspapers, whereas now there is a huge emphasis on social media and networking for job hunting.

About the market

- Reluctance to recruit someone older. Yes, we know discrimination on age grounds is illegal but we also know that this can play out in subtle ways
- Increasing numbers of public sector workers being laid off – flooding the job market and they are generally perceived as inflexible and lacking commercial skills.

The focus in coaching them

- Taking a step back and thinking about what they really want at this stage in their career rather than just trying to get another similar job, whilst recognizing that is fine if that is what they really want
- Suggesting alternatives they may not have thought about such as portfolio working, acting as a consultant or interim as a long- or short- term option, voluntary or charity work, especially if money is not an immediate urgency
- Helping them create their story in an engaging way which will boost their self-belief and give them a compelling narrative for their networking, impelling others to want to share in their success (Ibarra, 2003, Ibarra and Lineback, 2005)
- Helping them anticipate and then counter objections against employing them because of their age – in fact making their age an asset (Mays and Sloane, 2011)
- If they are interested in self-employment but fearful of whether it will work – giving them confidence and help them reduce their risks. Angela Watson of PDG Coaching

Solutions inspires others with her own story and also stresses that with the skills and experience of people in this age group the worst that can happen is they can go back to what they did before

- Helping them appreciate and sell their experience and skills and pulling that into a CV or business profile
- Developing their understanding of employer expectations, the job market and how to sell themselves or what it takes to be successful in setting up a business
- Developing their optimism and confidence.

Being part of a 'minority group': Ethnic, religious, sex or disability

Many of the points mentioned above apply to these groups as well in terms of challenges and coaching approaches so I won't repeat them here. Some people may face multiple disadvantages which you can support them in countering. In doing so you will need to add to your repertoire knowledge of organizations offering specific support to them and of relevant discrimination legislation.

This may also present challenges for you in your style and approach – for instance do you know how to coach someone with, say, Asperger Syndrome, Attention Deficit Hyperactivity Disorder (ADHD) or dyslexia? Get expert advice, help and information and use your supervision to consider the implications and any adjustments you may need to make in order to support them most effectively.

Psychological or behavioral challenges

Dealing with failure

The first question is 'When would you call something a failure'? One might take the NLP attitude of the 'belief of excellence' that 'there is no failure, only feedback' and that if you keep trying you'll run out of ways to fail – it was Edison who is alleged to have said that he had not failed 10,000 times (or was it 1,000, 700 or maybe 5,000?) but had just found 10,000 ways that didn't work, opening up the way to discover what *will* work.

So there is something to be said for reframing, and also for remembering that 'it's not over until it's over' as Deni Lyall says. Here are some coaching approaches to support your clients who are feeling 'a failure':

- *Reframing* – get them to see the event in a different light, one that is congruent for them and is not trite and simplistic. Ask questions so they see it from a different point of view, for instance, 'that wasn't the right job for them because it required someone who enjoys detailed analysis and that is not what they enjoy doing or are good at'. Possibly make suggestions if they are really fixed on a single, unhelpful point of view – but ultimately it has to be *their* reframe for it to have any power
- *It's not over until it's over* – a client of Deni Lyall's 'failed' an interview because he believed them when they told him it would just be a chat – it wasn't! He was totally unprepared and came across accordingly. At Deni's suggestion he went back to the interviewer, explained what had happened, was invited to another interview and got the job!

Resistant, won't engage, or feel stuck

Reasons and approaches here are much as you'd find with any coaching engagement. Here are some strategies you can use:

- As Deni says 'let's not make the person wrong'. It's about finding out what they *haven't* told you. Often it's something they are embarrassed about, such as, they failed at a recent interview, they can't position what they have done, their confidence has dipped through having lost their job and the longer it goes on the worse it gets. Often it's that they don't like networking. Whatever it is, it has to be talked about and you have to find a way to help them do so. Show you are on their side, respect them and that you can be trusted.
- A great question to ask, from Nancy Kline (1999): 'What's the assumption that's stopping you?'
- Use Clean Language: '. . . and when you are stuck, how would you like to be instead?' Then explore using the questions covered earlier.

- Talk about change models such as the Kübler-Ross change curve – remember, Karen Williams finds that by the third session strong emotions or feelings of frustration are common, especially for women, and understanding that this is normal helps.

They don't take action

I believe there's a lot we can learn here from Marshall Goldsmith's (Goldsmith with Reiter, 2008) research and experience on goal-setting and achievement. Here are the main reasons he cites and ideas on how you can get them moving:

- *Ownership* – is this really their own goal that they feel strongly about, or something that someone else wants for them? This is why a Well Formed Outcome (WFO) is so important in ensuring it's theirs and that they realize the effort required on their part to achieve it.
- *Time and effort* – it will probably take longer than they expect to achieve their goal and a lot more of their time. Manage their expectations and offer reassurance that this is not failure but just part of the process.
- *Difficulty* – it may turn out to be far more difficult than they expected, especially if it means changing identity and habits. They may need to work on themselves, as well as the practical aspects of job hunting or setting up a business.
- *Distractions* – the rest of life and work intrudes! The unexpected happens, priorities change. . . . Help your client be prepared for this and to prioritize or re-prioritize when it does happen. Help them feel OK about this – another reframe.
- *Rewards* – ensure your clients have short- as well as long-term goals or milestones and that they reward themselves for their achievements, however small. For instance the ultimate goal may be to get a higher-level role in another organization – this can be broken down into: researching and developing a shortlist of companies; recognizing their experience, skills and value added; pulling that into a compelling CV; identifying networking opportunities;

going to a first networking meeting. Get them to develop their own rewards that really work for them: maybe a day out doing something they love, a bottle of champagne, a special meal – perhaps just taking a day off!

Manage their expectations upfront when you contract with them and these will be easier to deal with later.

Low confidence/self-esteem

Some approaches to increasing self-esteem and confidence:

- The word 'confidence' is something of a generalization and few people lack confidence in every situation, it's not a permanent state. So, find a situation or situations where they are confident and explore this using Logical Levels (Dilts, 1990). This demonstrates that confidence is possible for them. They can then walk through the Logical Levels again to explore the situation where they want to have more confidence and find out the differences. Confident experiences can then be 'mapped across' to the others.
- For instance, a client of mine felt intimidated and tongue-tied with more senior managers, especially alpha males, but was full of confidence when speaking to colleagues or subordinates. Walking through the Logical Levels she realized that when she went to talk to someone senior she started to focus on their superiority and her inferiority, as she saw it. Using CBC she learnt to recognize this feeling when it started to develop and to replace it by thinking of them as her equals.
- In *The Secrets of Successful Coaches* (2011) Karen Williams interviewed Blaire Palmer, Executive Coach, author and formerly a top news producer for the BBC. When Blaire realized that 'high-up' people had the same squishy insides as the rest of us, it made it so much easier. Karen finds many people can relate to this analogy.
- Cognitive Behavioral Coaching – see Chapter 5.
- Use a variation of Perceptual Positions (O'Connor, 2001). Ask them to identify someone they know rates them highly, person A. Get them to step into the shoes of A and, speaking to themselves, say all the qualities about them they admire.

- You can follow this by asking them to affirm the same things about themselves, perhaps while looking into a mirror. 'I am . . . courageous', 'I am . . . funny and engaging' and so on. Be prepared for tears – this can be very profound.
- Explore confidence or self-esteem using Clean Language to find their positive metaphors.
- Recommend books which will further help their development, such as Gael Lindenfield's *Super Confidence* (2000) or *Overcoming Low Self-Esteem* by Melanie Fennell (2009) – these will act as a background to aid their understanding and supply exercises they can use.

Expect too much from you, either action or support

- It's important to manage their expectations at the start, so contract well and remind them of this if you need to.
- Talk to them about Transactional Analysis (Harris, 1969), the Parent, Adult, Child interplays, and the related Karpman Drama Triangle of Victim, Persecutor, Rescuer (Karpman, 1968). It's possible they will have these relationships and play these 'games' (Berne, 1964) in other parts of their life if they are trying to play them with you. Discuss this with them. Break the cycle by getting them to take responsibility for themselves – you may need to do some self-reflection and coaching as well about the responsibility *you* are taking and how you have contributed to the situation.
- Use tough love, some straight talking, pointing them to strong messages about what it takes to succeed.
- Ask powerful questions and give them space to think about them – such as, what do you believe about our relationship? What assumptions are you making about coaching? What will it take for you to do this yourself? Develop a 'Thinking Partnership' (Kline, 1999) with them.

Identity issues

Behaviors, beliefs and capabilities will be shaped by the way the client sees themselves and the identity they have adopted. And indeed their identity may be challenged or changed by events such as redundancy and other life changes. They may or may not be conscious of this. Use techniques discussed earlier to support them in ensuring their identity is in keeping with what they want to achieve, for instance Logical Levels (Dilts, 1990)

How about you?

So how about you in all this, faced with these difficult situations? Ensure you look after yourself – talk to your supervisor, take some time out for reflection and relaxation. Do ask yourself how you may be contributing to the situation but also ask whether the dynamic between you and your client is just not right (which does happen) or even whether they are not coachable by you or anyone else.

Key points from this chapter

- There are factors associated with particular transitions that make them particularly challenging, for instance redundancy or redeployment, being young or older, or being a senior executive.
- There may also be challenges associated with psychological or behavioral characteristics of the individual client which may be long-standing or develop as a result of their career transition experiences.
- You need to be able to draw on a range of coaching techniques and approaches – these are transferable from other coaching situations and you may also need some specialist knowledge, for instance about disabilities.
- You need a good understanding of what is going on in the world and where and how they can find further information for themselves.
- If your coaching or the relationship is not working, do some self-reflection and take the issue to supervision to get to the root of the problem. It may lie with the client or you may be contributing to it in some way. Either way there is useful learning and maybe even an acceptance that some people will not respond to the coaching you are able to offer or are even uncoachable at present.

Transition into a new role or life

So they think it's all over (with apologies to Kenneth Wolstenholme). Your client has made it into their dream job, or at the very least into the next step in their career. Or some broader change has been completed around them (such as when a company reorganizes or one merges with another) and they *find* themselves in a new role. As we have discussed, this is just the start of *another* career transition, the transition into a new role or even a new life – it may seem the transition is complete but there is a whole new world to adapt to at this point with both physical and psychological implications. We have arrived at stages 3 and 4 of the career transition model in Figure 2.1:

3 *Get new role/set up business*: preparation for first 100 days – business and personal vision and objectives
4 *First few months' transition*: successes, challenges, new identity and style, crystallization of new approaches, capabilities and skills, adapt to a new reality.

What *does* this new world want of them? (This is a favorite question of Professor Peter Hawkins' as you will see later.)

Often this is not even acknowledged as a career transition but what I and many other coaches know is that when we are called in to coach someone, more often than not there is some form of transition or even transformation that needs to happen. Our coaching can speed up that change, make it less painful for all concerned and ensure that people who could and should be highly effective quickly are not left to flounder or fail to reach their potential. Yet we are often only invited in once the person, team or organization has started to struggle, or not at all.

Witness Guy Buckland, who is now the successful Head of Learning and Development at a major law firm, on what happened to him earlier in his career:

> I moved from a Senior Sales Management role (out in the field, where my primary focus was on delivering to clients' needs through a team of people) to a Head of Learning and Development role, delivering projects that improved capability to large numbers of staff – I saw these people as my clients. What I failed to realize was the importance of managing stakeholders (who I should have seen as my clients!) and, more to the point, I wouldn't have known how to do that even if I had realized how important it was. The guidance I got was non-existent, and although I did a pretty good job and my performance was always rated as excellent, I didn't enjoy it, in fact I got quite disillusioned.
>
> When an opportunity arose to leave on voluntary severance I seized it, and other organizations got the benefit of my skills, learning and experience and I got to do L & D in another company, which I really enjoyed. And they paid me to go!

An important factor for Guy was that his psychological contract (Wellin, 2007) had been broken – a really significant career driver for him.

Coaching will speed up and reduce the pain of transition into any new role but particularly in the following situations:

- Stepping up in management and leadership
- Survivor syndrome – when a number of colleagues have been made redundant, leaving those remaining to pick up the pieces, deal with their guilt and their colleagues' work
- Being part of a merger or acquisition
- Going from employment to self-employment or from self-employment (back) to employment
- Retirement.

Stepping up in management and leadership

This must be one of the most significant transitions because of the number of other people also affected by the individual. What are the challenges for them and how can you help them?

Peter Hawkins, Professor of Leadership at Henley Business School and Emeritus Chairman of Bath Consultancy Group, has identified four stages in the development of leadership capability and he sees this very much as a *team* game, not an individual activity.

- *Stage 1:* trying to be a 'super manager'. Where you aim to manage all the parts and be an expert in every silo you are responsible for. This is characterized by problem solving, fixing things and keeping many plates spinning.
- *Stage 2:* the 'team leader' phase, where you start to realize you need to step back, focus on collective goals and not individual KPIs. The stress is on goals that no one manager can achieve alone.
- *Stage 3:* the 'team orchestrator' who sees their role as creating the right connections: leader A with leader B, leader C with their stakeholders and so on. When their help is sought, they ask 'who do you need to talk to?' not 'how can I fix your problem?'
- *Stage 4:* the 'team coach' who asks 'how do I grow *my* capacity, the team's *individual* capacities and the team's *collective* capacity?'

This concept of a 'hierarchy' of leadership styles is to be found in his book *Leadership Team Coaching* (2011a) as well as *Coaching, Mentoring and Organizational Consultancy* (with Nick Smith, 2006) and in his chapter in *Supervision in Coaching* (Hawkins, 2011b). One abiding theme is of the manager and leader, not as an individual but as part of the *system* and developing the ability to have greater and greater impact on the system and its parts. At the peak is 'the alchemist', the Mandelas and Gandhis of our world who are not really employable in organizations, other than as non-executive directors. They are able, in the moment, to create 'paradoxical seizure', to blow the circuit of current ways of thinking.

Of course 'other brands of leadership dimensions are available' and you or your coachee may already have an approach you favor, such as Charan, Drotter and Noel's *The Leadership Pipeline* (2011), Collins' level 5 leadership (2001) or Rooke and Torbert's 'Seven transformations of leadership' (2005). As this is not a book about leadership and leadership development I don't propose to discuss any particular model in depth but to use Peter Hawkins' work, which I interviewed him about for this book, to prompt you in thinking about and asking tough questions about the challenges for your coachee and yourself.

So what are the implications of this 'progression' of leadership for career transition? One of the major ones in Peter Hawkins' view is that the very thinking that makes you successful at one level of leadership makes you *un*successful at the next, meaning the leader has to *un*learn skills rather than learn new ones. We also looked at this in Chapter 6 in relation to the work of Furnham (2011).

Peter's experience is that during this time of career transition we *under*focus on what we need to be less attached to and give up. He likens it to the 'Eye of the Needle', the ancient gate in Jerusalem which was so narrow that camels could only pass through if all their baggage was removed. Every leadership transition – be it from operational to team leader, team leader to division, director to corporate or corporate to board – all have an 'eye of the needle' and leaders need to get clear about the baggage they need to drop each time.

What does this mean for you as a career transition coach? Peter has identified three themes:

1 Start thinking in terms of collective leadership rather than individual.
2 Help them see what they need to *unlearn*, to develop new insights. It is hard to see the mind-set you are currently operating in. He cites the example of one of the 'Big Four' accounting firms where people were asking him 'What do we need to do to reach Partner? What are the seven steps?' Peter's answer? 'The first step is to stop asking that question!' This is the Alchemist answer to a Technician question (Hawkins, 2011b). Leadership requires one to

ask, 'What difference do I want to make and how do I set about doing it?'. You don't get to be a leader with a technician mindset

So how do you confound the current mind-set? By setting them a task which they can't achieve from their current way of thinking and operating. Help them to use the transition to move to a new mode of operating in themselves.

3 Focus on the first 100 days and how they will make them a success. This starts before they walk in on the first day and there are certain things that can only be done during that time, for instance, making a first impression. After three months newcomers will already start to become inculcated into the system. It's a balance and they need to go in as a 'collaborative enquirer', not a new broom; honor what is there, listen – or they will build up resistance. On the other hand, don't take too long to decide to make changes or it will be too late to take advantage of your newness. As coach, help them to get this balance right. In his book *Creating a Coaching Culture* (2012) Peter includes a process and has also helped develop a workbook through Bath Consultancy Group (www. bathconsultancygroup.com) to assist in this.

So how do you get into an organization and help their leaders to make these career transitions successfully? This is tricky and can't usually be done on an individual basis for the very reasons discussed above – most of us don't know the shift we need and so there is really no point in asking individual coachees what they want. Peter uses a great opening question to trigger something new: 'What is it that the world is asking you to step up to?' And if you as a coach are going to be able to ask this and other questions which will shift their thinking it is no use *you* being of a 'technician coach' mind-set – you need to up *your* game. As Peter puts it – at least one person in the room needs to have a different mind-set so it had better be you!

How can you help your coachee discover what the world is asking them to step up to? Maybe 360-degree feedback or three/four-way contracting including their boss might work, but this is still problematic if those people also have a technician mind-set. Other questions to ask are: how will this organization get maximum value from this coaching? what different way of operating will come of it? Ask their boss a question they cannot easily answer. What's the transition the world is knocking on the door, telling you it wants that you're not hearing yet – it's future back, outside in. Development happens when the world comes and delivers a new lesson. During the first 100 days a new leader can often answer what the challenges are but not what that asks of them – that shift is transformational, a radical shift in thinking and being, is fundamental to the organization and requires unlearning on both sides. In Peter's view it can't be driven by a leadership competency framework.

How do you demonstrate a Return on Investment (ROI) for your leadership career transition coaching? In *Creating a Coaching Culture* (2012) Peter cites the coaching work of Ernst & Young. It was taking their new 'Direct Entry Partners' 18 months to reach the level of income generation built into the business case for recruiting them. We are talking about revenue levels of one to two million pounds. If that could be reduced to nine months it would be worth half to one million pounds to the company for every newly recruited Partner. New Partners were mostly coached by internal coaches and making use of some of the Bath Consultancy Group's 'first 100 days' materials. A key focus was the relational shifts that needed to happen. Much of the reason for the long lead time was due to the culture – a mind-set that automatically reacted against anyone trying to bring in the ways of others of the Big Four and a culture of 'heroes' – they were given a desk and a phone and told to get on with it.

To sum up, help them to 'start with the end in mind' (Covey, 1989) and reflect on how they can let go of previously successful mind-sets, how to be a collaborative inquirer, and how to use the transition to move to a new mode of operating in themselves. For those clients who want detailed practical help, you can refer them to something like *Harvard Business Review*'s Leadership Transitions CD-ROM, their collection Developing First Time Managers (which includes a CD-ROM, toolkit, books and articles covering a whole host of management challenges), or the Bath Consultancy Group workbook.

Survivor syndrome

It is now well recognized that there are physical and psychological impacts on those who are left after major redundancy exercises and in effect a career transition for them. Gerry O'Neill at Penna knows the psychological impact can be damaging to both the individuals and the organization, leading to reduced productivity, poor customer service, team conflict and sickness absence, so he aims to build this into the package of measures offered by a good employer. This was borne out in a 2009 survey by IRS Employment Review (Murphy, 2009) which found that the potential savings from job reductions were reduced by the impact on those remaining due to poorer performance and attendance, and increased staff turnover. However, these impacts can be mitigated by proactively engaging with and supporting those remaining – another significant business opportunity for the career transition coach.

At best, jobs and relationships will have changed and those who have kept their jobs often experience feelings of fear, insecurity and betrayal, especially if they have seen colleagues treated badly. And of course they probably have to take on the workload of those who have left as well as their own, plus they need to adapt to their new roles, understand their new customers and build new networks.

Services Penna offers include workshops and/or coaching for managers to help them understand and deal with these reactions and consequences, for instance introducing them to the change curve, appreciating the importance of communications and engagement and helping them develop the interpersonal skills to handle them well, e.g. conflict management, listening and empathizing.

It's important that managers are equipped to deal with this, rather than sending in a coaching or counseling team to deal with individuals, as they are the ones who will be working with their teams in the longer term. The benefits are increased credibility of the managers themselves and higher trust in the organization and its senior management.

Mergers and acquisitions

There are also opportunities to support organizations with integration of employees after a merger or acquisition, a sort of reverse outplacement according to Gerry O'Neill: another 'unsought' career change. Helping people adapt to cultural differences such as the degree of autonomy of managers, or simply the practicalities of bringing two companies together – developing new relationships, integrating into a new team, developing ways of working from the two different approaches. Organizations tend to be good at the processes of merger, acquisition and integration (such as IT, helpdesks, etc.) but not this people side. Again, there is a role for coaches in equipping managers to deal with the issues within their teams such as new behaviors and performance expectations, dealing with their hopes and fears and engaging them in the new environment.

Employment to self-employment/portfolio working or from self-employment (back) to employment

Autonomy, uncertainty and social isolation are key features of self-employment in whatever form that may be. Developing their awareness of these characteristics and their ability to handle them are major areas for coaching in these transitions.

In their article 'A grounded theory of portfolio working: Experiencing the smallest of small businesses', Clinton, Totterdell and Wood (2006), although focusing on portfolio working, draw lessons for all forms of self-employment. They found that those three psychological processes affected the individual's work intensity, well-being and work–life balance. Along with personal and situational characteristics these played a significant role in their experience of self-employment. In the absence of an organizational structure the self-employed need to develop and be aware of their own organizing principles or reference points for developing, making sense of and living their new identity, way of working and way of life (Gold and Fraser, 2002).

We have explored these in earlier chapters on decision making about self-employment – but now they are real and your coachee is living the experience, and finding, reviewing and refining their new strategies. No matter how well they have prepared there will still be an element of change curve.

When moving from self-employment to employment it's the loss of the positive side of these characteristics which can be painful – especially as this is often a move made reluctantly, for instance where a business has failed to produce the desired level of income or where an individual finds themself in need of a regular, guaranteed income each month. The loss of autonomy, freedom, flexibility, choice, being accountable to others, the organizational politics can be a severe shock to the system. Once again this is a significant change curve to deal with, and appreciating the gains and mourning the losses can be part of this process the coach can help with.

Retirement

Here again support with both practical and psychological matters is important. Retirement is increasingly meaning different things and happening at different ages, especially with changes in pension rules, reduction in pension benefits and the removal of default retirement ages.

Clients need to think about the obvious question of their finances, and much of this is easy for them to research themselves these days. The psychological transition is often far more difficult – in Gerry O'Neill's experience the loss of social interaction is the most difficult aspect together with loss of status and identity, especially if leaving a senior position.

Stories and narratives can be useful in your coaching toolkit for your client to explore how they see themselves and their identity and how difficult they might find it to adapt. In "We haven't got a seat on the bus for you" or "'All the seats are mine': Narratives and career transition in professional golf", David Carless and Katrina Douglas (2009) explored how the stories two professional golfers told themselves affected their career transition out of the competitive arena. Christiana told 'monological performance-oriented' stories which were very much aligned with the culture of elite sport. This resulted in her having an exclusively athletic identity so that when she left professional golf she suffered 'narrative wreckage and identity collapse' which led to mental health problems.

On the other hand Kandy's narratives were 'dialogical discovery-oriented' which gave her a multi-dimensional identity and self. When she withdrew from tournament golf her stories and identity remained intact and she suffered few psychological difficulties.

Support your coachee by getting them to tell their stories and if necessary to develop new narratives and identities through this means. One coach I know who was exploring her own impending retirement found it very helpful when her coach said 'Of course you'll always be a coach . . .'. It highlighted to her that the identity and being of 'coach' were not just a way of earning a living for her and would not end with her formal retirement.

Key points from this chapter

- Many people do not even recognize that there is a transition involved in adapting to a new role or life once it has been attained. Failure to get support during this time can have long-term negative effects on individuals and organizations.
- It's vital to ask what this new world wants and expects. This can be a significant challenge for both coach and coachee because a whole new way of thinking and being may be required which may not be apparent from the existing state. Find the challenging questions to ask that have to be answered from a new way of thinking.
- Usually there is an element of *un*learning that must be done because part of what has made someone successful in one role may be unhelpful in their new one.

- Organizational changes mean that many people experience a career transition unprompted by them. Coaches can help in managing this positively and proactively by supporting the managers.
- Creating or accepting a new identity plays a major part and this is developed through stories and narratives.

What it takes to be successful as a career transition coach

So, you've decided you want to coach people through career transitions, you've read Chapters 1 to 7 and have a whole range of useful approaches and tools you can use – what else will it take to set yourself up for success in career transition coaching?

Here are some more essential parts of the jigsaw from the experiences of seasoned coaches. I'm going to look at:

- The options you have for working as a career transition coach – the business models
- Training and qualifications.

First let's take a look at the different options for your work and the pros and cons of each.

Business model options

There are essentially four alternatives:

1 Independent: your own business working with either individuals or organizations
2 Associate of or freelancer working with an HR, OD (Organization Development), coaching or outplacement consultancy/agency
3 HR Department, redeployment unit or manager inside a business
4 Educational establishment or other public body such as organizations providing services to Job Centres in the UK.

These are not mutually exclusive and many coaches, including myself, combine two or more of these in their business model.

Considering each of these in turn:

Independent coach working with individuals or organizations

You run your own business and are totally responsible for its success including deciding your business model, winning clients as well as delivering the coaching. You may work with individuals or establish contracts with organizations to provide career transition coaching for a number of their employees.

What are the benefits of this?

- You are in control of your own destiny – you decide your approach, clients you will work with and not work with, use all your own creativity.

Challenges and issues

- Need to spend significant and continuing effort in marketing and developing your business to find a constant supply of clients
- Can struggle financially as everything depends on you and it can be difficult to juggle business development and delivery
- Business can be unpredictable – feast or famine.

Pros and cons of working with individuals vs organizations

- *Non-productive vs fee earning time* – the ratio when working with individuals is far less favorable than working with organizations. You have to win, manage, travel to and coach clients one by one which can be far more time-consuming than, say, winning a contract through an HR department, managing the contract through a single individual and going into the business for the day to coach a number of clients.

- *Fee levels* – you are likely to earn more if you work with organizations as you have the opportunity to win contracts for coaching as part of a larger development package, for instance to coach all managers at a particular level or in a specific department. It may also include other development activities such as workshops and master classes. The focus is unlikely to be purely on career transition unless it's connected with some kind of restructuring or redundancy exercise.

  Fees tend to be higher if you are coaching higher-level clients and many organizations are starting to use internal coaches rather than external at lower management levels so the business opportunities for coaching at those levels are reducing unless you are providing specialist coaching, such as for redundancy.
- *Managing stakeholders* When working with individuals you have a 1:1 relationship with your clients with no other stakeholders to take account of – a simple and straightforward relationship less likely to cause conflicts and complications. Managing multiple stakeholders within a business – the coachee and perhaps the HR manager, the individual's manager – and meeting all their expectations is more challenging. Clear contracting is vital
- *Loneliness* It can be lonely if you work only with individuals, especially if you have some who drain your energy and make little progress with what they say they will do. If you work with organizations you will have some opportunity for interaction with others in the organization as well. In either case, an energizing and supportive network is vital or you may be better working in a partnership or as an associate if this doesn't suit you.
- *Choices about who you work with* Organizations may give you little choice about coachees you work with whereas you make your own selections with individuals. That said you may feel pressure to take 'bad business' just to have some business when times are difficult. However, as you become more experienced and your business grows you will find these people easier to identify in your initial discussion and you can choose freely whether to work

with them or not or how to manage your and their expectations. As with any other form of coaching there are clients who make little or no progress. You'll also find that as people get to know you as the expert you will attract more referral clients and they will have a better understanding of what they can expect.

- *Funding and payment* Individuals are usually funding themselves so you really have to demonstrate the value and put it in their terms – you could be talking about the price of a holiday, but how much more will they get from finding a career they love? You may wish to ask for payment up front if you are coaching someone you don't know.

  Working with an organization you will probably be able to get a better idea of their creditworthiness but you may have to work to their terms of business – check what these are as large companies often have notoriously long delays built into their contracts; it could be as long as 90 days. Negotiate the best deal you can, if possible build in late payment terms and chase up promptly if the money doesn't arrive on time

- *Managing client expectations* Some clients Karen Williams works with on her standard three-month program do not have a new job at the end – some choose not to, others are hanging out for the right job and we're currently in a very difficult job market. You need to be clear that you can give clients strategies, but not guarantee a job. Also that it will need significant effort on their part – are they willing to do what they might need to do to get what they want? One of Karen's clients failed to take any of their actions, turned down Karen's offer of interview preparation support – and not surprisingly was unsuccessful!

  Working with an organization they will expect some measures of success – see the section below on Outplacement for more guidance on this. You should ensure they are realistic and also that the organization meets whatever criteria you need to enable you to fulfill your side of the bargain.

*What it takes to be successful running your
own career transition business*

Now I should warn you that some of this is going to sound contradictory! Whilst having a niche is important, the key to success is being flexible and multitalented. This is what I mean:

Niche. Choose a niche and develop a clear view of your ideal client. For example, Karen Williams has identified her ideal career client as a 39-year-old woman named Sarah. She has two children and works full-time in a professional job (as a manager, accountant or teacher for instance). She realizes her fortieth birthday is coming up, that she has probably 25 more years to work and doesn't want to still be doing the same thing then.

This is a very tangible niche and something that clients easily understand if you develop a clear 'elevator pitch' as Karen has done: 'I help people who are made redundant or are facing career change to find a job they love'. That said, this will evolve and clients will take from it what they are personally looking for – Karen's more recent clients have been looking for something missing in their life which relates strongly to their career and she now works extensively with new business owners.

Angela Watson has taken the reverse approach. She says career transition never ends, and that life is like an experiment: get involved, see which bits you like and which you don't. When she left full-time employment and trained as a coach and trainer she didn't define a niche – she felt the world was too big for her to do that. Her initial focus was on doctors because her background was in health and now five years later her business has four strands: 'Careers After Forty' coaching, leadership development in organizations, coaching individuals and training in executive coaching/ NLP. It was only when talking to me for this book that she saw how her offerings fit together, and felt she was 'pulling the reins together, like work streams, threads'. When she read Herminia Ibarra's (2003) *Working Identity*, this struck far more of a chord for her than most books on career change – she was fed up with ten-point plans!

Have other strings to your bow. Having a portfolio of offerings is key to earning a good living as an independent coach – most coaches do more than just coaching and offer other services which provide more income streams and either provide the route into coaching or are taken up later as a result of an initial coaching contract. Often coaching is combined with consultancy, some other expertise from the coach's former life or a completely different business idea.

Whilst Karen Williams has a clear niche she also has other services she can offer. Career transition coaching can be the 'entry point' for working with clients who come to her by recommendation and referral – for instance Karen's background is in Human Resources and from her previous experience she's also able to offer recruitment services, personal profiling, and time or stress management training. She doesn't seek corporate work as these are not her core clients but she does accept work with them if it comes her way. Her broad knowledge and experience also make her more effective as a career transition coach as she has more approaches and tools to draw on than other life coaches and as she's developed her own business she increasingly provides business mentoring to solopreneurs.

I offer consultancy, leadership and management development and most frequently my career transition coaching is part of a 'package' involving leadership development or consultancy. For me most of my business is as an associate and I also do some work with my own organizational clients covering management and leadership training plus consulting in change management and HR as well as coaching.

Taking this to the ultimate, there is the opportunity to include coaching in a 'portfolio life' and combine totally different offerings – for instance Andy Britnell, 'Musician, teacher, mediator, coach and alchemist!' as he describes himself on his blog 'See a man about a blog'. Andy developed his social media expertise for his own business and now offers this to clients – helping them (including me!) to develop the strategy and focus for their social media usage and their skills in using it. His coaching skills come into play here and this is part of his USP; he is able to offer more than the usual social media skills training or technical support.

Appropriate online presence. Karen Williams has a very active website (http://www.selfdiscoverycoaching.co.uk/) which reflects her style and approach and matches the needs of the clients she is aiming to attract – people say they feel she's talking to them. She has a friendly and personal manner and talks about problems they are facing.

You also most certainly need to be active on LinkedIn and consider what other online presence you need in your marketing strategy. Unless you are an expert it will probably be quicker and cheaper to buy some expertise to help you – someone like Andy Britnell who can help you think through your strategy and decide the mix.

Face to face presence. As an independent coach, the business is very much about *you* and you need, especially if you are working with individuals, to put yourself out there – running workshops, speaking at networking meetings and conferences. People need to experience you to want to work with you. Michael Neill, interviewed by Karen Williams (2011), says that to demonstrate your worth you must be able to show a potential client that if they have eight ways to get stuck, you have nine ways to get them unstuck – then you will win every time!

Keep links with former employers and colleagues. Again these can be a source of work over time even if not immediately – the same principle as keeping in touch with former valued clients. They know what you can do and you already have a trusting relationship with them (assuming you left on good terms!). Karen has found that the entry point here is more likely to be that you offer an expertise you were known for while employed there and can offer coaching as a development from that work.

These connections often bear fruit in unexpected ways. Johnson's observation in *The Independent Consultant's Survival Guide* (2005) has always stuck in my mind – the people who say they will give you work when you are talking about starting out on your own will *not*! This certainly proved true for me but these conversations were still hugely valuable because they gave me confidence in my 'pitch' and a belief that I could 'sell' plus they led to other contacts. I had just caught up with a former colleague when he was asked to do some work in Sri Lanka – he couldn't do it so he introduced me to what has become one of my most valuable clients.

The moral once again – network, network, network! I won't repeat everything I said about this in Chapter 5 in relation to your clients, just go back to that – and take your own advice!

Transition to running your own business. This sounds a bit like 'physician heal thyself' for a career transition coach, telling you about successful career transition! What is best for you? How do you like to make decisions and make changes in your life? Again, take the same advice you give to your clients.

You don't have to go for a 'big bang' if you are moving from being employed to self-employed, you can make the transition gradually – perhaps reduce your working hours, take holiday time or take a part-time contract so that you can start marketing and build up clients. That was Karen Williams' approach. This means the business may grow more slowly but it does provide a cushion and reduces one of the key risks of self-employment. On the other hand you don't want too much of a cushion or you won't be motivated enough to go out and find work!

I was fortunate in that I had a long notice period. Fortunate yes, but I also made full use of that time to talk to other people who worked for themselves, meet those who might give me work and really start to see my identity as a self-employed person. In fact I had started to make the transition about ten years before! I joined a networking group of self-employed business women: I volunteered to talk on subjects I was passionate and knowledgeable about and I learnt about being self-employed. By the time I did it, it was a small move forward in the same direction, not a great leap off a cliff.

As Angela Watson says, changing career should not be 'taking the plunge', which summons up images of going underwater, water wings and swimming. Just walk down the steps!

The steps she took were:

1 Become self-employed
2 Set up business – PGD Coaching Solutions Ltd
3 Her first contract was as a freelance interim manager in the NHS at a hospital which she knew well and who knew her (her background – nurse and senior NHS manager) four days per week (same kind of role as her previous job but doing it from a position of independence and self-employment). This was the first step in changing identity
4 Started coach training and NLP training (one day per week for this)
5 The next contract was in the same hospital but she said she could only do two days per week as coaching work had started and they agreed
6 First coaching contract with NHS – coaching doctors coming to the end of their training and preparing for leadership positions and nurses into leadership roles
7 Then stopped management work and continued working with the NHS, facilitating leadership development centers and so on. . . .

Whether or not you subscribe fully to Angela's and Herminia Ibarra's philosophy and approach, flexibility, reinvention and going with the changing focus in the world and the economy are certainly keys to success. Angela's 'Careers After Forty' blog (www.careersafterforty.com), came about because she shared her own story with people she was already working with and they wanted to know how she did it. Once again, this shows the power of your own story to get others working with you – in unexpected ways.

Associate of HR, OD, outplacement or other consultancy

What are the benefits of this?

• Business development and marketing are done for you
• You can have a flow of work, though not necessarily frequent and regular, for the price of time spent relationship building

- You may be given a process or format to work with which saves you having to spend time and effort developing your own. You may be given training in this
- Some organizations provide additional skills training, often at low cost
- To a greater or lesser extent you have 'colleagues' to work with so it can be less lonely
- Working for an HR or OD consultancy, rather than outplacement agency, you have the opportunity of other kinds of work which increases the potential variety and volume of your work and may be more lucrative than pure career transition coaching
- You are not an employee so you can be more distant from office politics and you don't feel that you have staked everything on one organization – you can remain more independent and not afraid of losing your job – you have and can find other clients
- It's a low cost, easy to set up option. You don't need expensive websites and marketing – you just need to network.

Challenges and issues

- It's often easy to get signed up with a consultancy but then not be given any work – often they already have a pool of experienced, trusted associates they always call on. I have been signed up with one organization for over four years and not had any work through them despite my best efforts to keep in touch and develop a relationship with key people.
- Some organizations will expect you to give of your time and expertise for nothing, for instance to attend their training, help in developing business or managing client interfaces. This will not necessarily guarantee you any work.
- Fees are considerably less than if you won the business yourself – this is how you pay for the business development and so on which they provide. Some have a formula for awarding fees such as a percentage of the fee paid by the client, which varies considerably – it may be as little as one third. Others may pay a fixed amount which you may

be able to negotiate yourself, with others it's a standard rate.

- The amount of work and therefore fees you earn can be unpredictable, although some consultancies may use you regularly and fairly predictably several times a month or even week.
- You may be expected to deliver using their processes and tools, which can restrict your freedom, and they may require you to pay for training specified by them.
- It can be lonely – you're not really part of the organization, often you will work on your own and can easily be cast aside when times are tough. Ensure you develop a good support network of like-minded people and you will thrive! That could be face to face, for instance, by being part of a co-coaching group or joining a Jelly (getting together for the day with other home workers, http://workatjelly.com/), or through the internet and social networking sites such as Judy Heminsley's http://www.workfromhomewisdom.com/

What it takes to be successful as an associate or freelancer

- Flexibility and not being precious about following your own methods
- Accepting that you will earn lower fees in return for the services the organization provides you with, in particular the considerable time and effort of winning business
- Being happy to work under someone else's brand – some consultancies are open about the fact that they use associates, others expect you to present yourself as an employee
- Seeing this as the best of both worlds – you work for yourself yet are relieved of some of the responsibilities of running your own business such as marketing
- Assessing the cost benefits quickly – either by research or by your experience of dealing with the organization. Ask around in your network to find out how much work you are likely to get and how much time and effort you will have to contribute free of charge to get this. Otherwise

you can waste a lot of time and effort for no return. Be prepared to cut your losses – but nothing ventured, nothing gained!

One organization I had dreamt of working with for years before I set up my own business agreed to take me on as an associate, but I gradually began to realize the price – many days of unpaid training initially and ongoing, including practically a day's journey each way to the training venue, and they were *very* prescriptive about how the work was done. Sadly I decided to walk away – but boy did I feel good about myself when I did! Know when it's time to get off the escalator!

- Network, network, network! Get yourself known, keep up with potential clients you already know, keep up to date with what's happening in your business market, build a support network of like-minded people

Specific pros and cons of an outplacement agency

- Specialist organization with a clear niche – both you and clients are clear on the service offered.
- You have a brand and resources behind you – for instance Penna has a well-established reputation in the outsourcing market and useful resources and products your clients can draw on, for example a portal with specialist information, workshops on subjects such as self-employment.
- It is possible to be employed directly by an outplacement agency, meaning you have a regular income and work flow. Even as an associate you may be given the expectation of a certain number of days per week or month.
- A whole range of roles may be available, from conducting initial interviews, to running workshops on general or specialist topics (e.g. job search or self-employment) and dealing with clients at levels appropriate to your level of competence and confidence – from blue collar, through management to CEO.
- Training may be provided, sometimes at low cost. Even at market rates it will give you transferable skills and qualifications and save you the effort of researching a suitable provider.

- You have experienced colleagues in the same field you can draw on for expertise or simply to bounce ideas and problems off. This can really help to overcome the isolation of working as a freelancer as well as providing professional support.
- Accept that there may be quite a long timescale involved with some outplacement coachees and some may take some time to engage with you at all because of their reaction to their redundancy. For instance, some may not want to be there with you at all and may either need time to trust you or to get some failures behind them to be convinced they could do with some help. Some may even be clinically depressed and simply unable to engage and focus. Others may think they will be fine, e.g. in starting retirement, but find after six months that they want some help to adapt. Penna generally try to wrap things up within a year, with six to nine months being most common, but the trend is for the programs provided to be shorter than in the past.
- It's very rewarding when you support someone made redundant in picking themselves up and helping them move forward.

What it takes to be successful working for an outplacement agency

- Need to be trained in and follow their methods – if you are an associate you will usually have to pay for training and will not be paid for your time spent training.
- May be expected to have specific qualifications, e.g. NVQ level 6 in career guidance and development.
- You will frequently be dealing with people in emotional shock and distress, possibly with serious issues of confidence and self-esteem, having been made redundant. You will often be dealing with the depths of the Kübler-Ross change curve or people who feel like victims. Others are resistant because they have been 'sent' or just don't like the idea of coaching – they see it as being judged or fear losing control. You have to be able to handle these strong emotions.

- You need to satisfy multiple stakeholders – coachees, client organization and the outplacement agency – to name but three! Gerry O'Neill of Penna finds most organizations implementing outplacement programs want Service Level Agreements (SLAs) with a range of targets and metrics, such as:
  - working to a budget
  - developing and meeting a delivery schedule
  - quality measures, for instance attendees' feedback on interventions such as workshops or individual coaching sessions
  - outcomes – increasingly Gerry is emphasizing to client organizations that these need to be based on what the individual wants as not everyone plans to go immediately into a new job. It's important to contract with the coachee at the start, for instance, what they want to have achieved in three months. This might be that they are confident with their CV and talking about what they offer or know the type of job they want etc., but this can change as they progress
  - understand the motivations of different organizations for providing outplacement; this will shape the offering expected of you. Some may be offering it because they believe they have a moral duty and genuinely want people to leave feeling successful, some are really just putting a tick in a CSR (Corporate Social Responsibility) box
  - Gerry O'Neill is increasingly finding there are pressures on budgets, with Procurement Departments getting more involved and demanding reduced costs and value for money. At some point the value to clients may become questionable, e.g. a one day workshop on the A–Z of finding a job followed by an hour of coaching may raise more questions than it answers.
- You need to be knowledgeable about the market – which industries are buoyant in the geography, what skills are transferable from one to another.
- Also be savvy about where clients can find out about jobs available – jobsites, agencies, company websites. Deni Lyall recommends indeed.co.uk.

- Know that outplacement really can work – only 2 percent of people in the job market are receiving it.
- Develop a good network to which you can also refer your clients for information and advice, e.g. senior managers of big corporations if that is what your clients aspire to
- Don't expect to be particularly well paid – some people doing this type of coaching are not what you might call 'professional' coaches, that is, someone who is making a career out of coaching. They may have quite a niche role and not act as a coach in the fullest sense. Perhaps they have been a senior manager, have a particular specialism such as knowledge of a market sector, or have expertise in setting up in business and provide support specifically on this. They may have limited coaching training and don't necessarily do this to earn a living, for instance they may be easing into retirement. Also you may not be paid for all meetings you need to attend, such as the initial client meeting. The key is to be really focused and achieve the objectives of these unpaid commitments in the shortest possible time.

A day in the life of an experienced outplacement coach

Deni Lyall of Winning Performance is a highly experienced and professionally qualified coach. Part of her work is with an outplacement agency. These are some of her experiences.

Deni's first introduction to a new outplacement coachee is normally a call from the coach who conducted the initial meeting asking if she can take on a new client. Also speaking with them will give her many useful insights before ringing the individual to check out points from the notes, to find out what they want from their first meeting with her and to set this up. These meetings differ enormously; Deni asks the client what has happened, how they are feeling, their thoughts so far about what they want to do. Some have already decided and just want help with CV writing and interview preparation, others are far more complex. Essentially it is about exploring what they know and what you know.

She finds people are quite savvy and streetwise these days and have often changed jobs or even been made redundant before. She believes her role is changing and it is now not so much about her own knowledge of subjects as such but connecting the client to them, for instance, what is going on in the job market and knowing which information sources are reliable and which not. You have to be up to date with networking sites such as LinkedIn and what sources of information are sound and reliable.

Part of the reason Deni is so successful is that she has a bigger repertoire of tools than many – in particular drawing on the range of Clean Language and NLP tools and also McClelland's (1961) needs-based motivational model. She also understands that what each person wants and needs is different. There is no point in starting to work on CV preparation and interview skills until the person has confidence and self-esteem. She's also prepared to challenge them, for instance if they aren't being active enough. She says, 'you haven't got a lot going on, others have'. Even then some people will waste their outplacement time or not use it at all. And she accepts that sometimes it doesn't work. You are not the right person to coach that individual for whatever reason, and that's fine too.

Regarding managing the multiple stakeholders involved in outplacement, Deni says it's a blend, although it's always about finding what's best for the coachee. Normally meetings are face to face but increasingly she's using Skype and phone, which gives flexibility to both her and the coachee – again people are much more used to using such media these days.

Another major skill is in helping coachees ensure job offers land together wherever possible. Ethically and reputationally for the outplacement agency and herself it's important that the coachee makes their own decisions; where she helps is in enabling those to be robust decisions. Deni helps them to speed up or slow down offers, for instance by calling the company and telling them they have another offer, that they really want their job but need a definite answer today.

I love the way Deni summed up – all people have got is what they've got and all they can have is what's available.

Dreams are not always possible. Share the diversity and wonder and then be pragmatic. Deni calls outplacement coaching 'working at the coal face'; the fantastic emails she receives from people are what makes it worthwhile – good for the soul!

HR Department, redeployment unit or manager inside a business

Benefits

- You work as a permanent employee with all the usual benefits such as the resources of an organization, employment rights, guaranteed income
- You may be provided with training in career coaching subjects such as coaching skills and psychometrics, at the time and cost of your employer
- You will most likely be doing this as part of a wider role and so retaining and developing your skill, experience and network in your other field(s)
- This can be a useful stepping stone to some form of self-employment, gaining you skills, experience and reputation plus contacts in this arena
- You understand the organization so know what is possible internally in terms of careers change and development and redeployment
- You will have an internal network to tap into to help career changers
- There is the opportunity to develop your network and reputation to benefit your own career
- You may know the individuals you are coaching so be able to develop trust and make progress quickly.

Challenges and issues

- Pressure of other priorities in your wider role
- Possible lack of influence as 'familiarity breeds contempt' and external 'experts' tend to be valued and listened to more. This applies both organizationally and with individual coachees

- You may become a scapegoat or dumping ground, having people sent to you that no one else wants to deal with
- Your status and position in the organization may inhibit you and your coachees, especially if it is very hierarchical and particularly if you are their boss or subordinate. Coachees may find it difficult to share their true feelings or intentions
- If you are working in a dedicated redeployment unit you may be 'tainted' with the stigma of redeployment yourself. Sad to say, no matter how much logic says that it is no fault of the individual, when their job disappears there is often a suspicion . . .
- Again, if your role is redeployment you may have unrealistic targets to meet, especially if there is cultural resistance from managers to filling their vacancies with redeployees
- Some redeployees may be reluctant to put in the personal effort needed to find another role and some may be unsuited to opportunities available, either due to attitude or capability.

What it takes to be successful as an internal career transition coach

- Prioritize to ensure you are able to integrate this with other work, negotiating with your manager if necessary
- Measures of success – ensure any targets or objectives are realistic (see above under the outplacement section for ideas). Set your own measures of success whether or not you have company targets
- Ensure you have the skills and training required
- Develop and use your network
- Use co-coaching and supervision to support yourself at all Logical Levels
- Be prepared to be tough where necessary, especially with redeployees for whom finding another role is a requirement rather than a desire
- Check, with yourself and the coachee, whether you are the best person to coach them if you are in a hierarchical relationship to them.

- Coach on other subjects as well if possible so you have broad experience and reputation. Many organizations are developing their internal network of coaches.

Educational establishment or other public body

As we go to press, revolutionary changes are taking place in the arena of careers advice, information, guidance, counseling, coaching. . . . This array of names is itself an indication of the state of play. The impetus for change is coming from a number of directions and whatever I say here is likely to be very quickly out of date. Therefore I am going to point you in the direction of a source of further information – as you would do your coachees!

The Careers Professional Alliance (CPA) is developing a single voice for careers education, information, advice, guidance and development. A new professional body, the Career Development Institute, is also under development.

As discussed above, career development qualifications are becoming increasingly important and the CPA's objective in the UK is to raise the professional standards of all career development professionals, assuring quality and public confidence in career development services.

So *caveat emptor*! Please check the CPA website (http://www.icg-uk.org/careers_profession_alliance.html) for information, and you can register with them as a Career Development Professional. Registration is open only to those with a specified level of CPA-approved career development qualification.

I will just add here that traditionally careers guidance has been predominantly the preserve of women and unfortunately regarded as lower status and less well paid compared with, say, leadership coaching where more men are involved. Perhaps these changes in perceived professionalism will alter some of those perceptions and indeed the realities.

What training and qualifications do you need?

Just as the debate continues around qualifications and regulation for coaching in general, so there is discussion about what should be required for career coaching. As can be seen above, the drive is intense in the public sector. One can imagine that before long a higher level of demonstrated professionalism all round may be demanded and even a mandatory qualification, especially when dealing with disadvantaged groups such as NEETS (Not in Education, Employment or Training). Currently there is a huge range of providers of outplacement and careers services, from public sector organizations to those in the private sector, such as Penna, offering well-established, tried and tested services, through recruitment agencies offering outplacement in response to economic circumstances, to one-man bands and simple online CV services.

Gerry O'Neill is currently running the newly developed OCR NVQ level 6 (degree equivalent) qualification in career guidance and development for career consultants at Penna. His view and that of others in the outplacement field is that this will become the minimum standard. This clearly has significant time and cost implications for those wanting to practice in the field although Gerry has found that even the very experienced coaches pursuing it have said they are really benefiting from this 12 to 18 month competency-based program. There are also questions of whether coaches should be able to practice while pursuing it, but equally, how would they demonstrate competency if they are not practicing?

So how do you decide the route to take?

As you've seen, there are pros and cons to whichever business model you choose and many ways of developing it over time. In choosing your initial route you will need to take account of your own career history – your current level of skill and experience in both coaching, career transition and other subjects which may form part of your business proposition. It also needs to reflect your own preferences and personality – whether you prefer structure and focus, whether you like to experiment and see how things emerge, whether you enjoy marketing and sales, for instance.

The critical thing is to go through exactly the same process as you would with a career transition client! Above all network, network, network – in particular talk to coaches involved in career transition and find out what has worked, and what hasn't worked for them. You'll really short-cut your learning and find out as quickly as possible what's going to work for you.

You might combine coaching with other totally different occupations as part of a 'portfolio life' – as a life and work choice as Andy Britnell has done, or as part of a transition from employment to full-time self-employment.

A successful career transition coach has many tools in their toolkit and is continually adding to their skills in either coaching or other fields and getting feedback on their performance, for instance through co-coaching.

This also differs from other types of coaching in that you do need knowledge of the subject, particularly of reliable sources of information. In the future you may need to hold specific qualifications in career transition coaching, especially if you want to work with vulnerable people or in a well-known outplacement organization or public body.

Key points from this chapter

- A whole range of business model options is open to career transition coaches including all forms of self-employment and employment, in the private and public sectors, and also a combination in a portfolio life.
- Specific qualifications in career coaching are set to become increasingly important, especially in the public sector.

Final word
Vital considerations

No matter what your specialism, as a coach there are some basics that apply, such as coaching ethics and contracting, the importance of professional bodies, training, accreditation, Continuing Professional Development (CPD) and supervision.

This chapter is a summary of these in the context of career transition coaching.

Coaching ethics and good practice

These are hot topics these days; all of the professional coaching bodies have their own statements of ethics and conduct which you are expected to follow as a member. You can read these online on the organization's website. In addition the ICF, for instance, run regular teleclasses on the subject of ethics to help you develop your practice. In most cases it's sufficient to follow these without the need to develop your own code and coaches simply refer to these in their contracting documents. However, you may feel there is a need with a particular client or coachee to add something more specific, for example about confidentiality and how and in what circumstances it applies.

One of the thorny issues when coaching in organizations is the confidentiality in the three- or even four-way relationship between you, your coachee and the line manager/Human Resources. This can be particularly acute when the organization, for instance, wants to place redeployees in new roles quickly.

Even with the existence and practice of these guidelines there is room for debate about what constitutes ethical and unethical behavior. In 2010 *Coaching at Work* magazine conducted a 'Poor Practice' survey of its readers and the members of a number of coaching professional bodies (Hall, 2010b). The aim was to capture what respondents thought constituted poor, incompetent or unethical practice and the extent to which they had encountered it. Whilst in some cases there was a very high degree of agreement, for instance 91 percent thought 'breaking client confidentiality' unethical, 'failing to contract' was seen as poor practice by 76 percent.

It's essential to keep up to date with current views on ethics and to take ethical and practical dilemmas to supervision.

Contracting

Probably the main pitfalls for career transition coaching lie in the need to manage expectations and the question of *who* you are contracting with and for what purposes.

Turning to the first of these, how do you ensure the coachee's expectations are realistic about what they can achieve in a relatively short span of your coaching? For example Karen Williams talks of helping a coachee to be better equipped to find a job at the end of the coaching relationship, but not to guarantee that they will find a job in that timeframe. Ensuring the coachee tests out and is realistic about what they want and are clear about what their part is in the deal and what is yours – these form part of both material and psychological contracting for Deni Lyall and Gerry O'Neill.

The dilemmas of the 'contracting triangle' and how to handle them were explored earlier with Gerry O'Neill – how to manage the relationship, expectations and confidentiality between yourself, the coachee and the client organization, especially where redundancy and a pressing need (on whose part?) to find a job may be involved.

Professional bodies

Yet another challenging decision! Whether to join and if so, which one? In terms of professional value and credibility there may be little to choose between them and it's largely a matter of your preferences – how the organization matches your own style, whether the learning opportunities they provide are practical for you or meet your learning preferences, whether you want more of a local or an international focus and so on. *Coaching at Work* magazine published a useful analysis in January/February 2010 which could be a useful starter (Hall, 2010a), although be aware of course that the bodies are continually improving and reinventing themselves as the profession develops so this will get out of date. It's easy enough to do your own research – through your network (physical or online), by reading the organization's website or trying out one of their events.

Training and qualifications

Training by any reputable coaching training organization will equip you with skills, tools, techniques – and more. Many general courses include elements of career transition coaching. Coaching buyers and coaching organizations are increasingly expecting training, qualifications and accreditation, especially those in or dealing with the public sector. As a career coach, in addition to your skills as a coach, you do need knowledge about employment and self-employment and to be able to give, or point people in the direction of, the information they need.

Training specific to career transition is currently the subject of debate and is set to become increasingly available, if not required. Once again use your network to find training that is credible and will suit you best. You can take your career coaching training to the level and in a format that suits you – if you want a recognized and specifically career coaching focused route in the UK there is the OCR NVQ level 6 (degree equivalent) qualification in career guidance and development (see OCR website, http://www.ocr.org.uk/qualifications/type/qcf/ad_gui/cgd_l6_dip/). Or, for instance, the University of East London offers Post-Graduate Certificate/Diploma/MA courses.

Another starting point might be the ICF's 'Training Program Search Service' on its website, which enables prospective students to search for ICF-approved training. But 'buyer beware' – make enquiries of those you know and trust when making your final choice and before spending large amounts of money!

Increasing your range in different practices/disciplines of coaching is also useful – you will have noticed I draw extensively on NLP in this book. You might want to enhance your skills in, say, Cognitive Behavioral Coaching.

My belief is that the greatest benefit will come to your clients if you use whatever you are drawn to that can serve them, and is congruent and authentic for you. In practice you will tap into many schools of thought – in fact the more you are confident with, the better coach you will be and the more able to support a wider range of people, with different thinking styles, experiences and so on.

Accreditation

Accreditation is evolving as the profession grows and further establishes itself. There is more to this than just training; you will need to demonstrate your credibility and capability in a number of different ways. Again, check what is required by the different professional bodies and which best suits your background, learning preferences and what you believe your clients will be looking for.

Continuing Professional Development (CPD)

Numerous enticing avenues are open to you – this is one of the things I love about coaching, it appeals to my passion for learning and there is just so much out there. Your CPD should address the different facets of your life and business as a coach and these can be found through, for instance:

- *Professional bodies* – have so much to offer. They provide training, often online such as teleclasses, master classes, local groups and face to face meetings and more

- *Co-coaching* – independent or run under the auspices of professional bodies such as the Association for Coaching
- *Conferences* – again, independently organized, by professional bodies or educational establishments
- *Professional journals – Coaching at Work, Choice, Coaching: An International Journal of Theory, Research and Practice*, for instance
- *Training or specialist organizations* – you'll find these through numerous sources: academic institutions, specialist coach training providers or organizations that focus on particular techniques and include training in their portfolio, for example, Clean Language, gestalt.

  Specific to career coaching there are specialists, such as John Lees, who provide training and master classes to add to your portfolio. Again choose carefully, master classes are for the experienced coach wanting to enhance their career coaching capabilities, they are not designed to teach you the basic coaching skills
- *Supervision* – essential to keep you ethical, fresh – and sane! You can take your pick from a variety of options – 1:1, group, face to face, teleclasses – whichever suits you best for practicality and style. Organizations are starting to expect you to receive supervision from an accredited supervisor so bear this in mind when making your choice.

Key points from this chapter

- The same best practice applies to career transition coaching as to any other coaching specialism. Your practice in career transition is just an overlay requiring some specialist approaches.
- Increasingly you are likely to be required to demonstrate your competence in the field of career transition coaching through training, qualifications and accreditation.
- Use your network to keep up to date and discover your best options to support you in both the overall and specialist requirements of career transition coaching.

So that's it!

I was reflecting on an appropriate ending for this book and thought it would be fitting to conclude with my own story of the career change that led to my writing it. Yes, you might have guessed it was to do with NLP. It's six years ago now and it's the story of an emergent career transition – I was unhappy in my corporate life when I went on Sue Knight's NLP Business Practitioner course and was inspired by Sue's own story. In particular the way she tested out what she wanted to happen appealed to me – when she wanted to move home she started spending more time in the location she was thinking of going to; I knew that 'trying it out' would work for me too. So by the end of the course when I did my presentation assessment I had a 'signature tune' for my career change in Simon Webbe's 'No Worries' – I just *knew* my life was gonna change . . . but I didn't quite know how or when. The next year I made that change; having experimented with it, tried it on for size, I grabbed the financial cushion which was the final piece of the jigsaw.

Whether you have read this book from cover to cover or dipped into chapters or tools that interest you, I trust you have found some gems that will serve you in your own career quest and in inspiring and supporting others to have meaningful and successful lives.

Do share your learning, achievements, questions and insights with this stimulating community of coaches and career changers at http://www.facebook.com/Caroline TalbottLtd and https://twitter.com/carocatalyst

References

Association for Coaching (2012) Coaching defined. Online. Available HTTP: <http://www.associationforcoaching.com//pages/about/coaching-defined> (accessed on 13 July 2012).

Bandler, R. and Grinder, J. (1975) *The structure of magic*, Palo Alto, CA: Science and Behavior Books.

Bateson, G. (1972) *Steps to an ecology of mind*, Chicago: University of Chicago Press.

Beckhard, R. (1969) *Organisation development: Strategies and models*, Reading, MA: Addison-Wesley Publishing Company.

Berne, E. (1964) *Games People Play*, London: Penguin.

Blunt, J. (2011) 'Successful career coaching', *The Bulletin of the Association for Coaching*, 6: 23–25.

Bohm, D. (1994) *Thought as a system*, London: Routledge.

Boudreau, J. W., Boswell, W. R. and Judge, T. A. (2001) 'Effects of personality on executive career success in the United States and Europe', *Journal of Vocational Behavior*, 58, 1: 53–81.

Bridges, W. (2004) *Transitions: Making sense of life's changes*, Cambridge, MA: De Capo Press.

Bridges, W. (2009) *Managing transitions: Making the most of change*, London: Nicholas Brealey Publishing.

Brinkley, I. (2006) 'Defining the knowledge economy: Knowledge economy programme report', *The Work Foundation*. Online. Available HTTP: <http://www.theworkfoundation.com/Reports/65/Defining-the-knowledge-economy-knowledge-economy-programme-report> (accessed on 13 July 2012).

Brinkley, I. (2008) 'The knowledge economy: How knowledge is reshaping the economic life of nations', *The Work Foundation*. Online. Available HTTP: <http://www.theworkfoundation.com/

Reports/41/The-Knowledge-Economy-How-Knowledge-is-Reshaping-the-Economic-Life-of-Nations> (accessed on 13 July 2012).

Buckingham, M. and Clifton, D. O. (2005) *Now, discover your strengths: How to develop your talents and those of the people you manage*, London: Simon and Schuster UK Ltd.

Cantore, S. (2011) 'Coaching senior executives on career transitions', paper given at the University of East London conference on Careers Coaching: Using coaching for careers decisions and transitions, 17 May.

Carless, D. and Douglas, K. (2009) '"We haven't got a seat on the bus for you" or "all the seats are mine": Narratives and career transition in professional golf', *Qualitative Research in Sport and Exercise*, 1, 1: 51–66.

Casey, P. (2004) *Is self-employment for you? Anyone can start a business . . . only a few can sustain a business*, Bothell, WA: Hara Publishing Group.

CBI (2007) *Employability and work experience: A quick guide for employers and students*. Online. Available HTTP: <http://aces.shu.ac.uk/employability/resources/timewellspentbrief.pdf> (accessed on 30 January 2013).

Charan, R., Drotter, S. and Noel, J. (2011) *The leadership pipeline: How to build the leadership powered company*, West Sussex: Jossey-Bass Inc.

CIPD (2010a) *Learning and talent development survey*. Annual Survey report. Online. Available HTTP: <http://www.cipd.co.uk/hr-resources/survey-reports/learning-talent-development-2010.aspx> (accessed on 30 January 2013).

CIPD (2010b) *Real-world coaching evaluation: A guide for practitioners*. Online. Available HTTP: <http://www.cipd.co.uk/hr-resources/guides/real-world-coaching-evaluation.aspx> (accessed on 30 January 2013).

CIPD (2011) *Learning and talent development annual survey*. Annual Survey report. Online. Available HTTP: <http://www.cipd.co.uk/hr-resources/survey-reports/learning-talent-development-2011.aspx> (accessed 30 January 2013).

CIPD (2012) *Employee Outlook*, Autumn. Online. Available HTTP: http://www.cipd.co.uk/hr-resources/survey-reports/employee-outlook-autumn-2012.aspx (accessed on 26 March 2013).

CIPD and YouGov (2010) *Shared purpose: The golden thread*. Survey report. Online. Available HTTP: <http://www.cipd.co.uk/

hr-resources/survey-reports/shared-purpose-golden-thread. aspx> (accessed on 30 January 2013).

Clance, P. R. and Imes, S. A. (1978) 'The imposter phenomenon among high achieving women: Dynamics and therapeutic intervention', *Psychotherapy Theory, Research and Practice*, 15, 3: 241–247.

Clinton, M., Totterdell, P. and Wood, S. (2006) 'A grounded theory of portfolio working: Experiencing the smallest of small businesses', *International Small Business Journal*, 24, 2: 179–203.

Collins, J. (2001) *Good to great: Why some companies make the leap . . . and others don't*, New York: HarperCollins.

Collins, J. C. and Porras, J. I. (2000) *Built to last: Successful habits of visionary companies*, London: Random House Business Books.

Costa, P. and McCrae, R. (1985) *The NEO Personality Inventory (NEO-PI-R) and the NEO Five-Factor Inventory (NEO-FFI) professional manual*, Odessa, FL: Psychological Assessment Resources.

Covey, S. (1989) *The seven habits of highly effective people*, London: Simon and Schuster UK Ltd.

Curwen, B., Palmer, S. and Ruddell, P. (2000) *Brief Cognitive Behavioural Therapy* (Brief Therapies Series), London: SAGE Publications Ltd.

Department for Education (2011) *NEET Statistics: Quarterly Brief*, November.

Dharma, M. Y. M. (2005) *Self-realization through pure meditation*, Yeovil, Somerset: Daoseva Press.

Digman, J. (1990). 'Personality structure: Emergence of the five-factor model', *Annual Review of Psychology*, 41: 417–440.

Dilts, R. (1990) *Changing belief systems with NLP*, Soquel, CA: Meta Publications.

Dilts, R. and DeLozier, J. (2000) *Encyclopedia of systemic NLP and NLP new coding*. California: NLP University Press. Online. Available HTTP: <http://nlpuniversitypress.com/> (accessed on 13 July 2012).

Dilts, R. and Gilligan, S. (2009) *The hero's journey*, Carmarthen: Crown House Publishing.

Dilts, R., Grinder, J., Bandler, R. and DeLozier, J. (1989) *NLP volume 1: the study of the structure of subjective experience*. Cupertino, CA: Meta Publications.

Dotlich, D. L., Noel, J. L. and Walker, N. (2004) *Leadership passages: The personal and professional transitions that make or break a leader*, West Sussex: Jossey-Bass Inc.

Drucker, P. (1992) *Managing for the future*, New York: Harper-Collins.

Dryden, W. and Neenan, M. (2004) *The rational emotive behavioural approach to therapeutic change* (Sage Therapeutic Change Series). London: Sage Publications Ltd.

Dunbar, A. (2009) *Essential life coaching skills*, Abingdon, Oxon: Routledge.

Erickson, M. and Rossi, E. (1992) *Hypnotherapy: An exploratory casebook*, New York: Irvington.

Fennell, M. (2009) *Overcoming low self-esteem: A self-help guide to using cognitive behavioral techniques*, London: Constable & Robinson Limited.

Fisher, J. M. (Revised 2012) 'Fisher's process of personal change', Businessballs.com. Online. Available HTTP: <http://www.businessballs.com/personalchangeprocess.htm> (accessed on 13 July 2012).

Fleisher, C. and Bensoussan, B. (2002) *Strategic and competitive analysis: Methods and techniques for analyzing business competition*, Upper Saddle River, NJ: Prentice Hall.

Francis, D. (1994) *Managing your own career*, London: Harper-Collins.

Furnham, A. (2011) 'The dark side of leadership: The role of the coach', paper presented at the Association for Coaching Leadership Conference, University of East London, London.

Gabriel, Y., Gray, D. E. and Goregaokar, H. (2010) 'Temporary derailment or the end of the line? Managers coping with unemployment at 50', *Organization Studies*, December 31, 12: 1687–1712.

Gattiker, U. E. and Larwood, L. (1988) 'Predictors for managers' career mobility, success, and satisfaction', *Human Relations*, 41: 568–591.

Gattiker, U. E. and Larwood, L. (1989) Career success, mobility, and extrinsic satisfaction of corporate managers', *Social Science Journal*, 25: 75–92.

Giang, V. (2012) 'Seth Godin: If you're an average worker, you're going straight to the bottom', *Business Insider*. Online. Available HTTP: <http://www.businessinsider.com/if-youre-an-average-

worker-in-this-forever-recession-youre-going-straight-to-the-bottom-2012-1> (accessed in January 2012).

Gilligan, S. G. (1999) *The generative self: A training workshop*, Santa Cruz, CA: NLP University Press.

Goddard, T. (2011) 'Promotion: Tips for getting your next career move', Tony Goddard Consulting. Online. Available HTTP: <http://www.tonygoddardconsulting.com/career-coaching/promotion—tips-for-getting-your-next-career-move/> (accessed on 13 July 2012).

Gold, M. and Fraser, J. (2002) 'Managing self-management: Successful transitions to portfolio careers', *Work, Employment and Society,* 16, 4: 579–597.

Goldman, A. (2006) 'Personality disorders in leaders: Implications of the DSM IV-TR in assessing dysfunctional organizations', *Journal of Managerial Psychology*, 21, 5: 392–414.

Goldsmith, M. with Reiter, M. (2008) *What got you here won't get you there: How successful people become even more successful*, London: Profile Books Ltd.

Goleman, D. (1995) *Emotional intelligence*, New York: Bantam.

Goleman, D. (1996) *Emotional intelligence: Why it can matter more than IQ*, London: Bloomsbury.

Goleman, D. (1998) *Working with emotional intelligence*, New York: Bantam Books.

Gratton, L. (2011) *The Shift: The future of work is already here*, London: HarperCollins.

Grove, D. and Wilson, C. (2005) 'Emergent Knowledge ΣK™ and Clean Coaching: New theories of David Grove', *The Model: The magazine of the British Board of NLP*, 2. Online. Available HTTP: <http://www.cleancoaching.com/#/clean-coaching-free-articles/4514711939> (accessed on 30 January 2013).

Grove, David J. and Panzer, B. I. (1989) *Resolving traumatic memories: Metaphors and symbols in psychotherapy*, New York: Irvington.

Groysberg, B., Kelly, K. and MacDonald, B. (2011) 'The new path to the C-Suite', *Harvard Business Review*, March: 60.

de Haan, E. and Niess, C. (2011) reported in 'Altered images', *Coaching at Work*, 6, 4: 34.

Hall, L. (2010a) 'Body talk', *Coaching at Work*, 5, 1: 34–39.

Hall, L. (2010b) 'Poor practice 2010 survey', *Coaching at Work*, 5, 4: 14–18.

Hamel, G. (2010) 'Capitalism is dead. Long live capitalism', *Wall Street Journal WSJ Blogs*, 21 September. Online. Available HTTP:<http://blogs.wsj.com/management/2010/09/21/capitalism-is-dead-long-live-capitalism/> (accessed on 13 July 2012).

Hamel, G. and Breen, B. (2007) *The future of management*, Boston, MA: Harvard Business School Publishing.

Hanh, T. N. (1975) *The miracle of mindfulness*, London: Rider Books.

Harland, P. (2009) *The power of six: A six-part guide to self-knowledge*, London: Wayfinder Press.

Harris, T. A. (1969) *I'm OK, you're OK*, London: Arrow Books.

Harrison, A. (2011) 'Young jobless "Neets" reach record levels', *BBC News*, 24 November. Online. Available HTTP: http://www.bbc.co.uk/news/education-15870240> (accessed on 4 February 2013).

Hawkins, P. (2011a) *Leadership team coaching: Developing collective transformational leadership*, London: Kogan Page.

Hawkins, P. (2011b) 'Expanding emotional, ethical and cognitive capacity in supervision', in Passmore, J. (ed.) *Supervision in Coaching*, London: Kogan Page.

Hawkins, P. (2012) *Creating a coaching culture* (Coaching in Practice series), Maidenhead: Open University Press.

Hawkins, P. and Smith, N. (2006) *Coaching, mentoring and organizational consultancy*, Maidenhead: Open University Press.

Howker, E. and Malik, S. (2010) *Jilted generation: How Britain has bankrupted its youth*, Oxford: Icon Books Ltd.

Ibarra, H. (2003) *Working identity: Unconventional strategies for reinventing your career*, Boston, MA: Harvard Business School Press.

Ibarra, H. and Lineback, K. (2005) 'What's your story?', *Harvard Business Review*, January. Online. Available HTTP: <http://hbr.org/2005/01/whats-your-story/ar/1> (accessed on 30 January 2013).

Institute of Leadership and Management/Ashridge Business School (2011) 'Great Expectations: Managing Generation Y', joint study, *People Management*: 64.

International Coach Federation (ICF) (2010) *Global Consumer Awareness Study*. Online. Available HTTP: <http://www.coachfederation.org/> (accessed on 13 July 2012).

Janz, T. (1977) 'The behavior-based patterned interview: An effective alternative to the warm smile selection interview',

Proceedings of the Annual Conference of Canadian Managerial Association.

Janz, T. (1982) 'Initial comparisons of patterned behavior description interview versus unstructured interviews', *Journal of Applied Psychology*, 67: 577–580.

Janz, T. (1989) 'The patterned behavior description interview: The best prophet of the future is the past', in Eder, R. W. and Ferris, G. R. (eds), *The employment interview: Theory, research and practice*, Beverly Hills, CA: Sage, 158–168.

Jeffers, S. (2007) *Feel the fear and do it anyway*, New York: Fawcett Columbine.

Jinks, D. (2011) Cognitive behavioural coaching for career transitions, paper given at the University of East London conference on Careers Coaching: Using coaching for careers decisions and transitions, 17 May.

John, O. (1990) 'The "big five" factor taxonomy: Dimensions of personality in the natural language and in questionnaires', in L. A. Pervin (ed.), *Handbook of personality theory and research*, New York: Guilford, 66–100.

Johnson, M. (2005) *The independent consultant's survival guide: Starting up and succeeding as a self-employed consultant.* London: Chartered Institute of Personnel and Development.

Johnson, R. W. (2009) 'Rising senior unemployment and the need to work at older ages', Urban Institute, Retirement policy program. Online. Available HTTP: <http://www.urban.org/publications/411964.html> (accessed on 30 January 2013).

Johnson, R. W. and Mommaerts, C. (2009) *Unemployment statistics on older Americans*, Washington, DC: The Urban Institute. Online. Available HTTP: <http://www.urban.org/url.cfm?ID=411904> (accessed on 13 July 2012).

Judge, T. A., Higgins, C. A., Thoresen, C. J. and Barrick, M. R. (1999) 'The Big Five personality traits, general mental ability, and career success across the life span', *Personnel Psychology*, 52: 621–652.

Kahn, L. B. (2009) 'The long-term labor market consequences of graduating from college in a bad economy'. Draft paper published on Yale School of Management website. Online. Available HTTP: <mba.yale.edu/faculty/pdf/kahn_longtermlabor.pdf> (accessed on 28 January 2013).

Kahneman, D. (2011). *Thinking, fast and slow*, London: Penguin.

Karpman, S. B. (1968) 'Fairy tales and script drama analysis', *Transactional Analysis Bulletin*, 7, 26: 39–43.

Kelly Services (2011a) 'Social networking changing the landscape for U.S. job seekers, Kelly Global Workforce Index™ Finds', 4 May. Online. Available HTTP: <http://kellyservices.mwnews room.com/press-releases/social-networking-changing-the-landscape-for-u-s--nasdaq-kelya-0751413> (accessed on 13 July 2012).

Kelly Services (2011b) 'The evolving workforce: Drivers of career choice and career progression'. Online. Available HTTP: <http://www.easyir.com/easyir/kellyservices/W1110_KGWI_CareerProg_final.pdf> (accessed on 13 July 2012).

Khoo, H. S. and Burch, G. St J. (2008) 'The 'dark side' of leadership personality and transformational leadership: An exploratory study', *Personality and Individual Differences*, 44, 1: 86–97.

Kline, N. (1999) *Time to think: Listening to ignite the mind*, West Sussex: Ward Lock.

Knight, S. (1999) *NLP solutions: How to model what works in business to make it work for you (People skills for professionals)*, London: Nicholas Brealey.

Knight, S. (2009) *NLP at work: The difference that makes a difference*, London: Nicholas Brealey Publishing.

Kotter, J. P. (1996) *Leading Change*, Boston, MA: Harvard Business School Press.

Kübler-Ross, E. (1973 [1969]) *On Death and Dying*, London: Routledge.

Lakoff, G. and Johnson, M. (1980) *Metaphors we live by*, Chicago: University of Chicago Press.

Latham, G. P., Saari, L. M., Pursell, E. D. and Campion, M. A. (1980) 'The situational interview', *Journal of Applied Psychology*, 65: 422–427.

Lawley, J. and Tompkins, P. (2000) *Metaphors in mind*, London: Developing Company Press.

Leary-Joyce, J. (2010) 'Power of personal presence: Gestalt coaching', teleclass for the International Coach Federation, 10 November.

Lees, J. (2006) *Take control of your career*. Maidenhead: McGraw-Hill Professional.

Lees, J. (2011) 'What's my line?', *Coaching at Work*, 6, 3 (May/June): 48.

Levin-Epstein, A. (2011) 'Job interviewing 101: 6 essential questions to ask every candidate', *CBSNews.com*, 5 December. Online. Available HTTP: <http://www.cbsnews.com/8301-505125_162-57336762/job-interviewing-101-6-essential-questions-to-ask-every-candidate/?tag=nl.e857> (accessed on 13 July 2012).

Levinson, M. (2008) 'Why Gen Y is unprepared to survive the recession', *Networkworld*, 4 November. Online. Available HTTP: http://www.networkworld.com/news/2008/110408-why-gen-y-is-unprepared.html (accessed on 30 January 2013).

Lewin, K. (1947) 'Frontiers in group dynamics: Concept, method and reality in Social Science; Social equilibria and social change' *Human Relations*, 1947, 1: 5–41.

Libet, B., Elwood, W., Wright J. R., Feinstein, B. and Pearl, D. K. (1979) 'Subjective referral of the timing for a conscious sensory experience', *Brain*, 102, 1: 193–224.

Lindenfield, G. (2000) *Super confidence: Simple steps to build self-assurance*, London: HarperCollins.

Lounsbury, J .W., Loveland, J. M., Sundstrom, E. D., Gibson, L. W., Drost, A. W. and Hamrick, F. L. (2003) 'An investigation of personality traits in relation to career satisfaction', *Journal of Career Assessment*, 11, 3: 287–307.

Luft, J. and Ingham, H. (1955) 'The Johari window: A graphic model of interpersonal awareness', *Proceedings of the Western Training Laboratory in Group Development*, Los Angeles: UCLA.

McClelland, D. (1961) *The achieving society*, New York: The Free Press.

McLeod, A. (2008) *Performance coaching: The handbook for managers, HR professionals and coaches*, Carmarthen: Crown House Publishing Ltd.

Macleod, D. and Clarke, N. (2009) 'Engaging for success: Enhancing performance through employee engagement', A report to Government. Online. Available HTTP: http://www.bis.gov.uk/files/file 52215.pdf (accessed on 13 July 2012).

McMahon, G. (2006) 'Doors of perception', *Coaching at Work*, 1 August. Online. Available HTTP: <http://www.coaching-at-work.com/2006/08/01/doors-of-perception/> (accessed on 13 July 2012).

McMahon, G. and Archer, A. (2010) *101 coaching strategies and techniques* (Essential Coaching Skills and Knowledge), Abingdon, Oxon: Routledge.

Marston, W. M. (2002 [1928]) *Emotions of normal people*, London: Routledge.

Mays, T. and Sloane, B. (2011) *Fifty and forgotten: How to find your next job when no one wants to hire you*. Online. Available HTTP: <http://www.optimarketllc.com/pdf/Fifty_and_Forgotten.pdf> (accessed on 28 January 2013).

Minghella, A. and Cooper, R. (1990) *Truly, Madly, Deeply*, film, Samuel Goldwyn.

Miniwatts Marketing Group (2001–2012) *Internet World Stats*. Online. Available HTTP: <www.internetworldstats/stats.htm> (accessed on 13 July 2012).

Mitterer, S. and Brice, N. (2007) *Brand alchemy*, Dublin: Blackhall.

Munnell, A. H., Webb, A. and Golub-Sass, F. (2007) *Is there really a retirement savings crisis? An NRRI analysis*, Chestnut Hill, MA: Center for Retirement Research at Boston College.

Murphy, N. (2009) 'Survey: Managing the survivor syndrome during and after redundancies', *IRS Employment Review*: 921.

Nicholson, N. A. (1984) 'Theory of work role transitions', *Administrative Science Quarterly*, 29, 2: 172–191.

O'Connor, J. (2001) *NLP workbook: A practical guide to achieving the results you want*. London: Element.

O'Connor, J. and Lages, A. (2004) *Coaching with NLP: How to be a master coach*, London: Element.

O'Connor, J. and Seymour, J. (2003) *Introducing NLP*, London: Thorsons.

OECD (2011a) Better Life Index. Online. Available HTTP: <http://www.oecdbetterlifeindex.org/> (accessed on 13 July 2012).

OECD (2011b) *Education at a glance 2011: Highlights*, OECD Publishing. Online. Available HTTP: <http://dx.doi.org/10.1787/eag_highlights-2011-en> (accessed on 18 July 2012).

Ofcom (2012) *The communications market 2011*. Online. Available HTTP: <http://stakeholders.ofcom.org.uk/market-data-research/market-data/communications-market-reports/cmr11/> (accessed on 13 July 2012).

Office for National Statistics (ONS) (2010) *Measuring what matters*. Online. Available HTTP: <http://www.statistics.gov.uk/CCI/article.asp?ID=2718> (accessed on 13 July 2012).

Oglethorpe, A. (2012) 'What qualities do you need to start up on your own?', *Taking the plunge* blog. Available HTTP: <http://www.businesszone.co.uk/blogs/antoinetteo/taking-plunge/

what-qualities-do-you-need-start-your-own> (accessed on 4 February 2013).

Paese, M. and Wellins, R. S. (2007) *Leaders in transition: Stepping up, not off*, Survey report published by Development Dimensions International. Online. Available HTTP: <http://www.ddiworld.com/DDIWorld/media/trend-research/leadershiptransitions_ang_rr_ddi.pdf> (accessed on 30 January 2013).

Palmer, S and Panchal, S. (eds) (2011) *Developmental coaching: Life transitions and generational perspectives*, Abingdon, Oxon: Routledge.

Passmore, J. (ed.) (2011) *Supervision in coaching: Supervision, ethics and continuous professional development*, London: Kogan Page.

Penna and CIPD (2008) *Gen UP survey: How the four generations work,* page 6. Survey Report. Online. Available HTTP: <http://www.cipd.co.uk/hr-resources/survey-reports/how-four-generations-work.aspx> (accessed on 30 January 2013).

Plimmer, G. and Schmidt, A. (2007) 'Possible selves and career transition: It's who you want to be, not what you want to do', *New Directions for Adult and Continuing Education*, 114: 61–74.

Priestley, D. (2010) *Become a key person of influence*, St Albans: Ecademy Press.

Prochaska, J. O., Norcross, J. C. and Diclemente, C. C. (1994) *Changing for good: The revolutionary program that explains the six stages of change and teaches you how to free yourself from bad habits*, New York: W. Morrow.

Rath, T. (2007) *Strengthsfinder 2.0: A new and upgraded edition of the online test from Gallup's Now Discover Your Strengths.* New York: Gallup Press.

Rooke, D. and Torbert, W. R. (2005) 'Seven transformations of leadership', *Harvard Business Review*. Online. Available HTTP: http://hbr.org/2005/04/seven-transformations-of-leadership/ar/1 (accessed on 26 March 2013).

Rosen, S. (1991) *My voice will go with you: The teaching tales of Milton H. Erickson*, London: W. W. Norton & Company.

Salgado, J. F. and Moscoso, S. (2002) 'Comprehensive meta-analysis of the construct validity of the employment interview', *European Journal of Work and Organizational Psychology*, 11: 299–324.

Schein, E. (1990) *Career anchors: Discovering your real values*, San Francisco: Jossey-Bass/Pfeiffer. Online. Available HTTP: http://

www.careeranchorsonline.com/SCA/startPage.do (accessed on 14 January 2013).

Seibert, S. E. and Kramer, M. L. (2001) 'The five-factor model of personality and career success', *Journal of Vocational Behavior*, 58, 1: 1–21.

Shepherd, J. (2011) 'Careers service and literacy hit by schools cuts and a dampener on aspirations: how pupils are paying the price of austerity', *The Guardian*, 27 December, pp. 1, 12–13.

Sissons, P. (2011) 'The hourglass and the escalator: Labour market change and mobility', *The Work Foundation*. Online. Available HTTP: <http://www.theworkfoundation.com/DownloadPublication/Report/292_hourglass_escalator120711%20%282%29%20%283%29.pdf> (accessed on 13 July 2012).

Starr, J. (2008) *The coaching manual: The definitive guide to the process, principles and skills of personal coaching*, Harlow: Pearson Education Ltd.

Sullivan, W. and Rees, J. (2008) *Clean Language: Revealing metaphors and opening minds*, Carmarthen: Crown House Press.

Tompkins, P. and Lawley, J. (2000) *Metaphors in mind*, London: The Developing Company Press.

TUC (2011) Report, *The Guardian Weekly*, 22 July, p. 17.

Weizer, S. and Stone, O. (1987) *Wall Street*, 20th Century Fox Home Entertainment.

Wellin, M. (2007) *Managing the psychological contract: Using the personal deal to increase business performance*, Aldershot: Gower.

Whitmore, J. (2009) *Coaching for performance: GROWing human potential and purpose – the principles and practice of coaching and leadership* (4th edition) (People Skills for Professionals), London: Nicholas Brealey Publishing.

Williams, K. (2011) *The secrets of successful coaches*, Leicester: Matador.

Wilson, C. (2007) *Best practice in performance coaching: A handbook for leaders, coaches, HR professionals and organizations*, London: Kogan Page.

The World Bank (2012) *Information and communications for development 2012: Maximizing mobile*; DOI: 10.1596/978-0-8213-8991-1; Online. Available HTTP: <http://www.worldbank.org/ict/IC4D2012> License: Creative Commons Attribution CC BY 3.0. (accessed on 18 July 2012).

Wray-Lake, L. (2011) 'Exploring the changing meaning of work for American high school seniors from 1976 to 2005' (Abstract), *Youth and Society*, August 8, doi: 10.1177/0044118X10381367. Online. Available HTTP: <http://yas.sagepub.com/content/early/2010/09/21/0044118X10381367> (accessed on 13 July 2012).

Yates, J. (2011) 'Keynote 2: Exploring the nature of coaching for career transition – Is it guidance by another name?', paper given at the University of East London conference on Careers Coaching: Using coaching for careers decisions and transitions, 17 May.

Index